Restore
Together

Urban Ministry in the Context of Technology and Energy In the 21st Century City

Dr. Louis J. Hutchinson, III

Foreword by Dr. William B. McClain

To
Deme, Naya, Louis IV,
Mom, Dad, Shane't, Kim
and those who endure

Drs Steph + Tom,

Because of your Ministry
I was able to write this
book. God has really used
the two of you TOGETHER
to touch so many. You are
more than just Des you
are truly life long friends.

We Love you very much. Thank
You, Thank You, Thank You!
Your Brother in Christ,

Acknowledgements

I want to thank my Lord and Savior Jesus Christ for sustaining and preparing me for a time such as this. I want to thank my Pastor, Rev. Dr. H. Beecher Hicks, Jr., First Lady Elizabeth Hicks and the entire Metropolitan Baptist Church family, where I learned to stand on the Word and under the Cross. I want to thank Rev. Colin Thorne and the First Baptist Church of Hyattsville where I interned as Assistant Pastor while in Seminary. I want to thank the New Union Baptist Church where I served as the Pastor for three years after finishing my Masters of Divinity Degree. I also want to thank those that are and will be a part of the Restoration Baptist Church where I currently serve as the Senior Servant and Pastor. And finally I want to thank the Wesley Theological Seminary faculty and community for stretching and fortifying my soul. Without the many trials, tribulations, triumphs, and lessons learned from these experiences this book would not be possible. May God be glorified!

Table of Contents

Abstract

The goal of this project was to create a digital ministry platform to enhance the church's ability to provide care and services to the community. The platform seeks to erase the digital/energy divide for the impoverished. That platform, developed and implemented here, is named "Restore Together Community," located at http://www.restoretogether.com .org or .net. It is dynamic, collaborative, multilingual and accessible to individuals with disabilities, and enhances an individual or organization's gifts/resources, ability to provide holistic counseling, discipleship, sharing of best practices, and ability to organize community action.

Foreword

There is an all-out assault on the poor. And that assault is global, systemic, digital, immoral and effective. And the church, whose responsibility it is to advocate for the poor, is in a "collective slumber." There is a Digital Secularization – the immoral use of technology that exploits the people, systems, and the social and natural environment across the world – in need of a humanizing, moral revolution. These factors and many others conjoin to make these very trying, desperate, and difficult times for the poor – and especially the growing numbers of urban poor of all ethnic and racial groups. But there is now a post-modern church technology prophet to appear to awaken those who sleep! And this truth-teller also writes! The great prophet of the poor of the last century, Dr. Martin Luther King, Jr., would be plenty proud of him and consider him in the same tradition of his "Poor People's Campaign" in Washington just prior to his death in 1968.

Louis Hutchinson comes along just in time to offer help. In this book he writes a sound sociological and scripture-based analysis, thoughtful theology, a deeply passionate love for the church and society, and a practical guidebook and project to foster a global digital ministry that calls for the collaboration of the church and the world for beneficial social change. And with clear and easy illustrations and demonstrations how technology can be pressed into service for the common good and with case studies showing the effectiveness of Restoring Community Together, we have the Internet as a prophetic voice. He helps the church to see how a digital ministry/platform community can use the Internet, laptops, desk tops, smart phones, iPods, iPads and other technology as tools that God has given us to benefit humankind across the world and all to the greater glory of God.

As one of his professors at Wesley Theological Seminary throughout his Master of Divinity and his Doctoral degree work, I have observed his development as student and scholar of theology and technology. I know that he has been far ahead of most of us in seeing the ways they can be brought together into spiritual, moral, and practical service to the benefit of us all.

His life's story – from the crowded apartment in the Bronx of New York as the oldest with two siblings with an abusive father, his own experience of poverty and homelessness and his conversion to Christianity – figure heavily into his passion to develop this project and to passionately seek a way for the poor to benefit from his work. His solid work in the larger society plays a role in his effort to help us see how the church and other institutions in society can and should be collaborative for the common good. It seems not a coincidence that he is the Pastor of a Baptist Church named: RESTORATION!

As we read his writing here, as we view the illustrations offered and the cases rehearsed and evaluated, I also feel the warm presence and quiet and tender support of a wife, Demetra, whom I have also been privileged to know and teach at Wesley Seminary, and a family and larger family I know who have urged and sacrificed for the time to come when this Project could be made available to a larger public. I joined my wife, Jo Ann Mattos McClain, long ago in urging that this book be published. She was all too glad to serve Lou as his initial consultant/editor. We are now all friends.

It is my fervent hope and unceasing prayer that this book will be received and read by many, and that that many will turn out to be most pastors and church leaders, as we join others in other institutions in the community in RESTORING COMMUNITY TOGETHER. I believe we can!

The Rev. Dr. William B. McClain
Mary Elizabeth Joyce Professor of Preaching and Worship
Wesley Theological Seminary
Washington, DC

Introduction

I was born in that most traditional definition of the city, Manhattan, New York, at Harlem Hospital on September 4, 1965, after three days of very difficult labor by my mother. I was born to a father who was a non-believer in a converted Jewish family and the oldest of 11 children, and a Protestant mother who was a strong believer, the second oldest but the leader of a family of six children. My father's family had converted from Christianity to Judaism while living in Charleston, South Carolina, and shortly thereafter migrated to New York when he was eight years old. As a result of his opposition to the conversion and other childhood hardships due to societal oppression, he lost his belief in God. I would be the first and oldest of what are now more than 80 grandchildren and great-grandchildren on both sides of my family. My parents ended up in apartments directly across the street from each other on Boston Road in the Bronx when they were ages fourteen- and thirteen-years old, respectively. My father's family lived in a two-bedroom apartment with both parents and eleven children, and my mother's family in a two-bedroom apartment with both parents and six children. For my first two years of life I lived back and forth between these two apartments, in very humble "manna-like" circumstances, financially.

Throughout my childhood and early adulthood I considered myself Jewish and was expected as the oldest of my generation to remain Jewish. There were relatives on my father's side of the family who were cantors. My Jewish grandfather, who "kept kosher," would often remind me that I was the leader of my generation and that if any of the younger grandchildren acted out of line, I would be held accountable. As my paternal grandfather had attempted with all of his sons, he urged me, according to Hebrew custom, to be as independent a man as possible by the age of 13. As early as I can remember, I had a strong spirit of discernment, and I would always speak out against injustice without consideration for self, but especially for someone weaker.

My maternal grandfather, from Trinidad, suffered with cancer upon my birth. I was told that he would hold me in his arms and read the Bible to me and pray over me for hours. Shortly after I turned three my grandfather, after suffering for several years, succumbed to his cancer. Shortly after his death, my maternal grandmother came to live with us. I can remember my grandmother teaching me about Jesus, against the will of my father. She would read the 23rd Psalm to me over and over again. We would wake up every morning to her singing of *Amazing Grace*, with her strong Barbadian accent, and to the aroma of her warm baked bread that carried her love throughout our home. Every morning as I would bite into her bread she would whisper to me before going off to school, "No matter what, never forget the Bread of Life, and don't you ever forget Jesus."

My maternal grandmother's repetition of the 23rd Psalm would anchor my soul forever. One day when I was eight years old I returned to what was now our Queens apartment after school. My mother was not yet home from work and my grandmother was speaking to me about God. Suddenly, my father yelled at her violently to stop immediately, and he approached me aggressively, asking me if God existed, and before I could answer he yelled at me that God did not exist. When I defiantly responded that God did exist, he hit me. He then asked me again to explain how God existed. I went on to explain that God was greater than the entire universe, that God created everything. He hit me again, harder. Then he grabbed my arm and he put me inside a very dark closet in the middle of the apartment and closed the door. The closet was pitch-dark – there was no light. For the first couple of minutes he stood outside of the closet door taunting me, "If God exists, let him get you out of the closet." After a few minutes he stopped taunting me but left me in the closet in total darkness for what felt like an hour. During that entire time in the closet I spoke to God repeatedly saying, "God, please protect me and my whole family; God, please protect me and my whole family; God, please protect me and my whole family." When my father finally let me out of the closet he asked me again if God existed. I looked at him and once again I said, "YES, God exists!" In a rage he sent me to my room for the rest of the afternoon. I now know and embrace the truth that oppression must be confronted with a forgiveness that affirms our unconditional love, thus the first of the seven last words from our Lord and Savior Jesus Christ saying, "Father, forgive them for they know not what they do!" We must hate the sin but love the sinner, as love will truly conquer a multitude of sins. Through love and faith, I have truly forgiven my father.

Both sides of my extended family believed strongly in the God of Abraham, Isaac and Jacob, and I therefore remember the establishment of a substantial prayer life at a very young age that would overcome the influence of non-belief in God that existed in parts of my family. It was a prayer life that allowed me to hear God through discernment and through dreams. Years later, after being called into the ministry, I would come to find out from my mother that when I was three years old she was approached by a man who seemed filled with the Spirit in the front of the apartment building where we lived on Davidson Avenue in the Bronx. She had never seen this man prior to being approached by him that day. The man would tell her that he was a Christian and that she needed to protect me and nurture me because I would be a warrior for Christ with a strong gift of discernment. He told her that I would speak out against oppression and injustice and that I would be a global pastor.

Throughout my youth, God did not prepare me in the traditional manner. Instead, God prepared me by instilling in me the ability to not rely on others for that which was being denied, to persevere and to look for the solution through faith and through God. God's strength and wisdom would use my earthly father as a tennis coach who would drive me and push me to shovel snow off of tennis courts in my youth in order to practice outside in freezing weather, because my family had no money for indoor court time in the middle of the New York winter. God's strength would later drive me, after finishing high school, to ride my bicycle 15 miles to Nassau County Community College for classes, and then another 8 miles to a 3-hour tennis team practice after class, and then another 5 miles to the United Parcel Service to load trucks late at night, and then another 15 miles back home, five days a week, in order to eventually receive a tennis scholarship to The George Washington University in Washington, DC. God's grace and mercy allowed me to live when many around me, including family members, were being murdered or imprisoned.

It was by faith that I left my family for the first time in my life to fly to Washington, DC, to attend The George Washington University on a tennis scholarship in January of 1985. After arriving at GWU as one of the first Black full-scholarship tennis players in the school's history, I learned that the housing office would not have a room available for me until well into my first semester. The teammate who had picked me up from the airport graciously offered me the box spring of his bed for me to sleep on in a very large closet in his dorm room for what ended up being 45 days. I remember the emptiness inside me and the valley of concern during that first night in DC. I did not share my reality with my parents. There was a small voice inside me that first night that said, "The test is not to the swift, it is to those who endure." That first night I thought about my maternal grandmother who had an incredible faith in God, and how she would go into the cabinet day after day, when there was no money, when there was no food, and she would find a way to bless us with a gourmet meal made from virtually nothing. I remembered how my grandmother could make a sardine sandwich taste like filet mignon at Morton's steakhouse. Hallelujah! Time after time I watched her face life-and-death situations, and with a peace that came from the Holy Spirit, she would sing *Amazing Grace* with a smile, knowing that God would make a way somehow.

After my first semester at GWU I would go to the computer lab to write computer programs late at night after studying and afternoon tennis team practice. Occasionally, there was a disabled and homeless man who would sleep in front of the computer lab building. This man would share the Gospel of Jesus Christ with me. He would encourage me to keep on pushing when I was exhausted. When he talked he would always praise God. He would say, "My Son, how are you doing this evening, praise God?" "Praise God, are you having a good day today?" And sometimes he would even say, "I am tired and I am hungry, praise God." Now at this point I still considered myself to be a Jew. But it was the Christian faith of my maternal grandmother that laid the foundation for me to stop and listen to this Christian homeless man. This man fed me faith when I was tired. He fed me hope when I was exhausted. He fed me Jesus. He exemplified an unwavering faith and belief that contradicted his circumstances. He blessed me with his faith and unconditional love.

Now it was four years later, after graduating from GWU with a degree in Computer Science/Statistics, and it was my birthday. I was working for a computer consulting company. I received the news that my maternal grandmother had a stroke. My boss at the consulting company called me in to her office and said, "I am sorry to hear about your grandmother, but unfortunately today is your last day." Within 45 days from that day, my grandmother died and, shortly after her death, I was evicted from my apartment. I was homeless.

I was much younger then and had been living beyond my means. The termination was unforeseen and unexpected. I remember getting emergency food stamps on H Street, NE, in Washington, DC, and getting daily odd jobs in order to survive, jobs like moving furniture in government buildings with men who had just been released from prison. I remember moving furniture one day for someone I had tutored while at The George Washington University as they looked on in astonishment, wondering why I was there. Every material thing that I had was lost. My spiritual foundation was shaken. I started to doubt. But once again I remembered my grandmother's faith. I remembered the homeless man at GWU years before saying, "In the time of trouble get down on your knees and pray." He had told me, "If you are down on your knees it is impossible to fall!"

And so, 23 years ago, I got down on my knees and I truly accepted Jesus Christ while broken, in a bathroom stall at Union Station in Washington, DC. I prayed and I said, "Lord I accept Jesus as my personal Lord and Savior, and if you hear my voice, and my pain, and my struggle, if you pull me out of this hole, if you deliver me, I will tell the whole world about Jesus and what you did for me!" This experience took place right before a scheduled job interview; I had borrowed enough money to get a one-way train ticket to go from DC to Boston for a job interview. I did not know quite how I was going to get back to DC after the interview. After an all-night train to Boston, I was interviewed by thirteen people in one day and was offered a job making three times my previous salary. I had only enough money for a one-way ticket to Boston, but through God's grace and faithfulness the hiring company paid for the ticket to get me home to DC. God is faithful and God is able!

In 2003, almost eleven years after accepting Jesus Christ as my personal Lord and Savior, after receiving the aforementioned job that took me from homelessness to work at Powersoft Corporation, the number one application development company worldwide, and then four years later to a job at Netscape Communications Corporation, the number one Internet company worldwide, four years after leaving Netscape/AOL I was the CEO of Crunchy Technologies, Inc., which would become one of the top three accessibility software companies worldwide, selling to many countries. While at Crunchy I did interviews with the *Washington Post*, the *Wall Street Journal*, Bloomberg Television and many major technology publications. I especially recall one night when Crunchy was facing what seemed to be an insurmountable obstacle: the dot.com bubble had burst and we were owed millions of dollars by a major customer. While prostrate on my bedroom floor I prayed and I wrestled with the Lord, arrogantly stating, "Lord, I cannot get through this without you, I need more than an angel, send Jesus down here right now!" I had no way of knowing that after this prayer, for three years both my wife and I would go without any income, losing our home, another investment property, one of our two cars, and having to sell furniture and our wedding gift watches to one another in order to survive. There were times when we lived off coins found deep down inside the couch. There were times when we were hungry, and there were times when we were afraid. But in the midst of it all we heard God, our faith grew, our obedience was fortified, and we both heard and accepted a call to preach the Gospel of Jesus Christ.

I was accustomed to the Lord responding to my requests through dreams, discernment and visions. The night after praying, "Send Jesus down here," I had an unexpected dream. In the dream I was on a train that was going across a long bridge that looked like the Bay Bridge in Maryland. As the train approached the end of the bridge, the bridge collapsed and the train hit the water and started to sink. The train car I was in started flooding, with water gushing up to everyone's waist, and above our waists there was an air pocket. Suddenly in the dream, everyone on the car looked at me, and I asked everyone to hold hands in a circle, and I started to pray, and then I started to baptize individuals on the train and I could see their souls resurrecting from their bodies to Heaven. When I awoke that night a joy, peace and a power saturated and engulfed me in a way that no words, pictures, gestures, expression or thought can accurately describe. I woke my wife, Demetra, and when I looked at my hands they were soaking wet, but the rest of my body was dry.

Now, I had prayed for assistance with the company. What was this dream about? I gathered enough courage to approach and describe the dream to the Rev. Melvin Maxwell in the sanctuary that Sunday after service at the Metropolitan Baptist Church in Washington, DC, where we were attending church. In haste, as he was exiting the sanctuary, he said to me, "Before you pray to the Lord for clarity, read Isaiah Chapter 6." And so that night, after reading Isaiah Chapter 6, I prayed to the Lord and I said, "Whatever you are trying to say to me Lord, here am I, send me!"

That night I had another dream. In this dream I was a white horse in the sky and I was battling against the enemy. Every time I would speak in the dream, my words would turn into arrows aimed at the enemy. In the battle, the enemy shot an arrow at me, and it hit me in what seemed to be my heart. But rather than dying, I exploded into millions and millions of white horses, engulfing the sky. Again, I awoke to a joy, peace and power that saturated and engulfed me.

The following Friday, after the Men's Bible Study at the Metropolitan Baptist Church in Washington DC, I approached Minister Donald Burrell, and I was in tears as I was becoming unraveled with this experience. He smiled and he said, "You are the most logical 'Spock-like' brother I know. Trust me, you are not losing your mind. Be prayerful at this time." That night I prayed once again, asking God why God had answered my original request about Jesus in this manner, to please give me absolute clarity. That night I had a final dream related to my calling. In that dream I could see myself lying lifeless in a coffin, eyes closed, arms crossed. Standing over me was a silhouette of Jesus. Watching this I could see myself clearly and I could see the silhouette of Jesus, but no matter what angle I struck in the dream I could not see the face of Jesus, just the silhouette. Then Jesus spoke: "Rise up and stay on the path that I have called you to do!" When I awoke, there was a peace, a power, a purpose and clarity that remains with me even today. I knew that God chose me to preach the Gospel, to share the discernment, to take prophetic action and to build an ark for the remnant through a global digital technology platform.

I believe that God prepared me for ministry throughout my life. As early as five years old, my father would have extensive dis-cussions with me about Descartes, Plato, Freud, Marcus Garvey, W.E.B. DuBois, Carter G. Woodson, Malcolm X, Martin Luther King, Jr., Albert Einstein and so many others involved in history, psychology, science and sociology and philosophy. My father was academically gifted – he had taken the Scholastic Aptitude Test in the 9th grade and got only one question wrong! It was common for my father to discuss many subjects and theories associated with these persons with me, and whoever else would listen. While my mother was also academically gifted, she sacrificed and spent tremendous time with me on my academic foundation, teaching me to read and write well before I was five years old. She taught me to exceed expectations, to overcome obstacles, to try harder, to burn the midnight oil if necessary. My mother was the first person who would make me understand the concept of *creatio ex nihilo* that dwelled in her and therefore in me. When my mother was in high school, she had two dresses that she would hand wash and rotate every day for four years, and two pairs of shoes for all of her activities, including church. On the first day of her typing class in her junior year, the teacher approached her and said that because she was left-handed and because she was the only student in the class who did not own a typewriter at home, then she would need to drop the class. My mother excused herself, and went into the bathroom to pray. After prayer, she returned to the class. She pulled out a piece of paper and she traced the keys from the typewriter on the paper. She refused to drop the class. She taught herself how to type by practicing at home on the traced keys on the paper night after night. Eventually she would receive an "A" in the class. Every time she told this story, she would emphasize that it was the God inside of her who would not allow her to quit or fail. She would tell us that God could create something out of absolutely nothing if we would just believe and then take action.

In 2012, years after coming out of the pitch-dark closet to proclaim to my father that God indeed exists, after getting down on my knees in a filthy bathroom stall and accepting Jesus Christ while praying for deliverance from homelessness, after fighting to survive three years with no income for myself or my wife, I praise God for God's grace, mercy and preparation! I am now a pastor with a Doctorate in Theology, with a tent ministry as an officer and Vice President at Exelon Corporation (NYSE:EXC) the largest competitive power generator in the United States. I have a wife whom I love dearly, my absolute soul-mate who is in the midst of pursuing a Doctorate of Psychology, and two extremely gifted and loving children. I now know that I am spiritually commissioned to scratch deeper than the surface toward a theology of social change throughout global urbanization; a change that eradicates oppression, racism, classism, hatred and so many other social illnesses, through active and collaborative participation in the unified chorus of suffering love, using the tools of technology, systematic theology and prophetic preaching.

CHAPTER ONE

Theology of the City

This chapter and book examines the city in the context of its now-ubiquitous definition, historical foundation and theology, and will focus on the challenges the city faces in the 21st century, with particular attention paid to the restoration, transformation, reconciliation and spiritual liberation of its inhabitants. The city can no longer be viewed solely through the confines of geography, population, socio-political makeup or commerce, for the definition of "city" in the 21st century far surpasses such limitations. The real-time establishment of the city is reflected in multiple scenarios; e.g., the on-line movement that impacted the 2008 U.S. presidential election; the virtual collaboration that has allowed Al Qaeda to survive and function globally; the 2010/2011 Arab Spring political uprisings throughout the Middle East (Syria, Egypt, Libya, etc.) aided by community activism using social media; the 2011 global Occupy Wall Street movement; the cyber security war that has replaced the cold war between global super-powers; the Fortune 500 organizations that ignore human suffering by succumbing to manipulation of unlimited virtual data, thus supporting their growing capitalistic investment in the prison-industrial complex; the digital divide that now impedes the deeply-impoverished from being able to apply on-line for employment at fast food restaurants and minimum wage jobs; communication through tweets and text messages that displaces intimate human interaction critical to forming meaningful relationships; and the virtual video games that desensitize a generation and gear them toward division and destruction rather than reconciliation and creation.[1]

---

1 Jürgen Moltmann, *Trends and Transmutations in Christology - Contradictions of Scientific and Technological Civilization: The Way of Jesus Christ*, 64.

The connected city has evolved into a dynamic, ever-changing organism that collaborates through a desensitized economic, physical, spiritual, and psychological normative gaze.[2] It is a normative gaze without compassion, steeped in real-time virtual apathy toward soul salvation. This normative gaze represents the struggle between observation and evidence; hence, there is systemic control of the oppressed through redaction of detailed measurement by the oppressor. This redaction of measurement serves the purpose of painting a distorted visual picture or first impression as representative of the entire truth and circumstance of the city. It is a gaze that simultaneously multiplies sin while giving sin the veneer of morality. In a matter of minutes, today's city can be connected through a few keystrokes, mouse clicks, or voice commands to a network of devices that communicates independent of class, language, culture, ethnicity or age to a vulnerable, desensitized and apathetic population of souls that is capable of derivative global chaos and spiritual incarceration when the love of God is not central and present. The new city has become an internet- and technology-driven virtual collective whose mind and voice must be radically renewed and transformed. This transformation is possible through a sacrificial willingness to restore "God's presence" to the tabernacle or temple at the center of this new city, independent of medium, for without God's presence in the temple there is *nihil negativum* (matter-less nothingness, absolute death), the city is barren, the prophetic voice silent, eternal salvation compromised and reconciliation not achievable. The church must be *creatio ex nihilo*, the prophetic light of reconciliation, the temple at the center of this new digital and global Internet city, through integrated restorative ministry that is active and present.

According to Karl Barth, *creatio ex nihilo* is creation by the Creator out of absolute nothingness. This absolute nothingness is the antithesis of the Creator and is the matter-less, evil, sinful nothing of nothing. It is the nothingness that was defeated by the Creator through the spoken Word in the beginning of the

---

2 Cornel West, *Prophesy Deliverance! An Afro-American Revolutionary Christianity,* 59.

Old Testament and through the birth, death, and resurrection of the incarnate Word in the New Testament. As stated by Barth, "Nothingness is thus the 'reality,' which opposes and resists God, which is itself subjected to and overcome by His opposition and resistance, and which in his twofold determination is the reality that negates and is negated by Him, and is totally distinct from Him."[3] According to Dietrich Bonheoffer, this nothingness is the nothingness that lies between the freedom of God and creation: "This nothingness therefore is not primal possibility or a ground of God; it 'is' absolutely 'nothing'."[4] For Bonhoeffer, the world existed in the beginning in the midst of nothing based on God's freedom. Jürgen Moltmann put a much greater emphasis on the pneumatology in his view of *creatio ex nihilo*, for he believed that when creating, God has no presupposition at all.[5] He establishes the word creation as 'bara' (create, not make) which is creation of the whole where there is no material needed to create. He feels that when God creates, to say "out of" is misleading, and that *ex nihilo*, which is pure nothingness, becomes something immediately. For Moltmann, when God creates in the new creation, God withdraws God's self in order to go out of self. Eternity breathes itself in, so as to breathe out the Spirit of life; therefore, the self-determination of the Creator, the Savior and the Spirit take place. This self-determination, a self-limitation, means making room for creation and making possible the liberty of the non-divine image of God in God. And so Bonhoeffer, Barth, and Moltmann acknowledge that in the beginning, God created out of absolute nothing. I further assert that in the beginning the triune God (the Creator, the Savior and the Spirit) defeated absolute nothingness by the reconciling action of creation, through God's presence and thought. I believe that the moment that God thought, God pulled out of God's self to create and defeat darkness, chaos, and nothingness and at that moment it was. Therefore, where God is not

---

3 Josiah Young, *Barth the Genesis Emphasis* (Lecture, Wesley Theological Seminary, Class Handout.)

4 Dietrich Bonhoeffer, *The Beginning: Creation and the Fall*, 34.

5 Jürgen Moltmann, *In the Beginning God Created: God in Creation*, 74.

connected, central or present, there can be no eternal creation or eternal life. But when God is present, when God is central in the midst of the city, when the church (the temple) confronts and does not avoid the tension of the city, the power of eternal life, liberation and ultimately resurrection will be achieved for souls waiting to be transformed and restored.

I concur with Moltmann that Christ's relation to His Father and His Father's relation to Him are pneumotalogical relations. While Christ is completely mortal in Himself, He can no more be severed from the Father and the Spirit than they can be severed from Him. Christ is therefore truly, or fully, or completely personal as the Father's incarnate Son.[6] And so, on the cross, Jesus empties Himself of His divinity; but His triune connection to God the Father remains through the Spirit who rests on Him in the mode of the Shekinah. Joining the Father and the Son, heaven and earth, eternity and time, life and death, the Spirit is both divine subject in Christ and the unity of the difference of the Father and the Son. "Where the Spirit is not active, Jesus cannot do anything, either."[7] The Father raises the Son through the Spirit, the Father reveals the Son through the Spirit, the Son is enthroned as Lord of God's Kingdom through the Spirit, and the risen Son sends the creative Spirit from the Father to renew heaven and earth in preparation for the *parousia* (the coming of the Messiah) and the *eschaton* (the coming of God). And so the Father then subjects everything to the Son, the Son transfers the consummated Kingdom to the Father, and ultimately the Son subjects Himself to the Father.[8] This is affirmed through the Gospel of John, Chapter 1:1-5 and 10-14:

> [1] In the beginning was the Word, and the Word was with God, and the Word was God. [2] He was in the beginning with God. [3] All things were made through Him, and without Him nothing was made that was made. [4] In Him was life, and the life was the light of men.

---

6 Moltmann, *The Way of Jesus Christ*, 75.

7 Ibid., 83.

8 Ibid., 93.

⁵ And the light shines in the darkness, and the darkness did not comprehend it. ¹⁰ He was in the world, and the world was made through Him, and the world did not know Him. ¹¹ He came to His own, and His own did not receive Him. ¹² But as many as received Him, to them He gave the right to become children of God, to those who believe in His name: ¹³ who were born, not of blood, nor of the will of the flesh, nor of the will of man, but of God. ¹⁴ And the Word became flesh and dwelt among us, and we beheld His glory, the glory as of the only begotten of the Father, full of grace and truth.

In summary, before there was anything God was and continues to be everything, and by God's humble entry and eventual sacrifice of self in the midst of darkness, there is grace and therefore salvation available to all. God's incarnate purpose is clear in John 3:16-17:

¹⁶ For God so loved the world that He gave His only begotten Son, that who so ever believes in Him should not perish but have everlasting life. ¹⁷ For God did not send His Son into the world to condemn the world, but that the world through Him might be saved.

Though Jesus was faced with defeating every obstacle the church will ever know, His supplication was unwavering, His resolve was eternal and His approach was bold. John 19:17-18, and 11:25-26 states:

¹⁷ And He, bearing His cross, went out to a place called *the Place* of a Skull, which is called in Hebrew, Golgotha, ¹⁸ where they crucified Him, and two others with Him, one on either side, and Jesus in the center.

And He fulfilled His promise from John 11:25-26 where He had previously stated to Martha:

> ^{25} "I am the resurrection and the life, He who believes in Me, though he may die, he shall live. ^{26} And whoever lives and believes in Me shall never die."

With all the opposition and relentless tension, Jesus was always central and Jesus was always present.

This dialectic tension between the church/temple and the city is also apparent in the synoptic Gospels of Matthew, Mark, and Luke. The presence of God (Jesus Christ, "the new temple") that entered the temple in Jerusalem is a reflection of God's incarnate infusion of self into the city in order to cleanse the temple building, the surrounding city and the people of the earth.[9] Conversely, the city is the place where Jesus is supported and not supported, identified and denied, and a place of crucifixion and resurrection. In the gospel of Mark, the city is antithetical to the temple yet unknowingly dependent on the new temple for derivative deliverance of its inhabitants. Throughout Mark's gospel, Jesus moves in and out of the city, establishing the metaphor for virtual global deliverance independent of geography, but as is true today, His presence was rejected by those placing emphasis on the material and non-sacrificial rather than the spiritual temple that must be central to our eternal lives. The Gospel of Matthew also determines that Jesus himself is the temple, and that the presence of God was no longer confined to Jerusalem. Furthermore, Matthew 23:21 states that the temple is the place where God dwells: be that Jesus, Jerusalem or Galilee.[10] But not unlike today, in Luke (19:41-44, 21:20-24) the city has turned its back on God and the presence of Jesus Christ at the center. In today's society, the temple or the church is not living up to its responsibility to be the clarion voice that cries out in the wilderness, the unified chorus of suffering love that will take bold prophetic action based on the presence of Jesus within each of us through the Holy Spirit. As the definition of the new city (the new Tower of Babel) attempts to expand through virtual omniscience, omnipotence, and omni-

---

9 P.W.L. Walker, *Jesus and the Holy City*, 13.

10 Walker, 27.

presence, why has the church not infused the presence of God in the center?

In the Old Testament there was the tabernacle which was a portable tent or sanctuary used by the Israelites as a place for worship during their early history that was created to be physically and spiritually central to their existence. The tent was built in accordance with God's instruction to Moses on Mt. Sinai during their years of wandering in the wilderness (Ex. 26:35). With the people contributing labor and materials from Egypt, the tabernacle was completed to God's specifications. The tabernacle was a tool used by God to begin transformation of not only the Israelites' material items from Egypt, but also their hearts and discipline associated with Egypt. God blessed their handiwork by covering the tent with a cloud and filling the sanctuary with His glory (Ex: 40:34).

After the tabernacle there was Solomon's Temple, also known as the First Temple. It was the temple in Jerusalem, on the Temple Mount (also known as Mount Zion), before its destruction by Nebuchadnezzar II after the Siege of Jerusalem of 587 BCE. According to the Hebrew Bible, the temple was constructed under Solomon, king of the Israelites. This would date its construction to the 10th century BCE. During the kingdom of Judah, the temple was dedicated to Yahweh, the God of Israel, and housed the Ark of the Covenant or the presence of God. Once again this temple was central to the physical and spiritual existence of the children of Israel in the city.

And now we find ourselves with the greatest gift, the living temple, Christ's body for in John 2:19-21:

> [19] Jesus answered and said to them, "Destroy this temple, and in three days I will raise it up." [20] Then the Jews said, "It has taken forty-six years to build this temple, and will you raise it up in three days?" [21]

But Jesus was speaking of the temple of His body. And He has imposed a great responsibility on those who have proclaimed from their mouths and believed in their hearts that Christ died, was buried and was resurrected, for in 1 Corinthians 6:19 it is stated:

> [19] Or do you not know that your body is the temple of the Holy Spirit who is in you, whom you have from God, and you are not your own?

And further in 1 Corinthians 3:16-17 this great responsibility is extended to the church:

> [16] Do you not know that you are the temple of God and that the Spirit of God dwells in you? [17] If anyone defiles the temple of God, God will destroy him. For the temple of God is holy, which temple you are.

And so with this great responsibility, when faced with insurmountable obstacles on earth, why do we continue to forfeit our heavenly authority and power? In Luke Chapter 7: 18-23 the scripture says:

> [18] Then the disciples of John reported to him concerning all these things. [19] And John, calling two of his disciples to him, sent them to Jesus, saying, "Are you the coming One, or do we look for another?" [20] When the men had come to Him [Him being Jesus], they said, "John the Baptist has sent us to you, saying, 'Are you the coming One, or do we look for another?'" [21] And that very hour He cured many of infirmities, afflictions, and evil spirits; and to many blind He gave sight. [22] Jesus answered and said to them, "Go and tell John the things you have seen and heard: that the blind see, the lame walk, the lepers are cleansed, the deaf hear, the dead are raised, the poor have the Gospel preached to them. [23] And blessed is he who is not offended because of Me."

Are we the church or is there another? This synoptic Gospel of Luke preaches to all of us. It preaches to the church. It preaches to believers who are rich beyond measure in Jesus Christ, yet living as beggars; only because we choose to pretend that we are ignorant. We have yet to accept our wealth, for we are still living as spiritual paupers; refusing to pro-actively engage in Kingdom-building initiatives at the forefront of the challenges that we face in the new city. We are fearful that we might lose something or fail, and so we remain lethargic in doing the work that God has called us to do. Drawing upon our eternal spiritual endowment, we as Christians have all the resources needed for living to build God's kingdom "to praise the Glory of His grace," right here on earth, through a willingness to stand up to destruction, death, defeat, and all things antithetical to God in the city.

But where is the voice of the church and those who dwell therein? When is the last time we wept, not only in the moment, but days after witnessing a stranger's unjust pain or discomfort? For we, the church, cannot sit back and idly watch, hoping that vulnerable human minds will be transformed by police response to violence in our cities, that human trafficking will dissipate without us, God's servants, being put in harm's way; that abject poverty will be neutralized; the hearts of greedy executives on Wall Street will change; bombs being dropped by robotic planes killing innocent thousands in the Middle East will stop; and that no reluctant soldiers will come home to homelessness or incarceration, as the oppressed and disenfranchised continue to look to us for help. After all, are we not the deputized restoration agents that God has filled with God's Holy Spirit? Why do we squander the power that God has placed inside of us? Why do we ignore history and the Holy Spirit?

For thousands of years, the city has struggled to "convert power into form, energy into culture, dead matter into living symbols of art, and biological reproduction into societal creativity."[11] History has proven that a city cannot function unless it has the means and the will to create new institutional arrangements to cope with the ever-changing energies that are presented. In the midst of neo-

---

11 Lewis Mumford, *The City in History*, 30.

colonialism and global capitalism, the city is still confronted with overcoming the challenges that form a negative and dominant symbiosis.[12] As far back as the cities of Mesopotamia and Egypt, urban populations established creative ways to control flooding, repair environmental damage, store and control water, and operate mass communication and transportation, while establishing forms of criminal justice that defined guidelines to achieve order in those cities.[13] But simultaneously there have always been destructive forces in the city such as war, slavery, and dehumanizing oppression. Capitalism in the city has evolved to focus solely on profitability, divorcing itself from social responsibility. Unlike religious sanctions embedded in past city structures, there is no longer a central religious presence guiding the moral direction of the new city. There is no voice standing at the center of the new city that will sacrifice life and limb to push back the capitalists, the oppressors, the apathetic, or the *nihil negativum* in order to awaken the collective conscience of the un-awakened. Instead there is only a collective slumber, a normative gaze that embraces or ignores oppression in the name of the material reward of the moment.

Far too often, the individual and collective church or the modern temple is weak in its comprehension of its responsibility as authentic and uncompromising restoration agent for all stakeholders impacted by the moral atrocities of discrimination and oppression that are often overlooked in the new city. In the context of oppression in the city, the oppressed, when not consciously striving toward the common goal of reciprocal restoration, increase the likelihood of being the involuntary oppressor at some point. Through the assertive leadership of the church, when holistic forgiveness and restoration is sought by all stakeholders there is an opportunity for crucified and honest discovery that may shed light for all to realize that more often than not, the oppressor is the oppressor because of a sustained oppressive experience. It may also reveal to the oppressed the lurking

12 Mumford, 568.

13 Mumford, 410.

vulnerability of quickly transitioning from being the oppressed to becoming a derivative oppressor; thus, the cycle of oppression.

It has become clear that there must be praxis through a committed effort of reconciliation between the church and the new city. And the entire community must come together through the church to embrace the least- and most-impacted of these. Ultimately the challenge to the church and the new city is a willingness to submit to transformation at the point of greatest weakness, which upon submission will begin the foundation toward an egalitarian metropolis.[14] This metropolis is "a social, political, and spiritual context that is preoccupied with justice, the mutual affirmation of persons, ecologically uplifting and safe, and where love and respect are the order of the day. It is an environment where true compassion, reconciliation, restitution, and right relationship are taken seriously as public policy."[15]

Howard Thurman addressed well the urgency of oppression and the Church's central responsibility in his book, *Jesus and the Disinherited*:

> This is a matter of tremendous significance, for it reveals to what extent a religion that was born of a people acquainted with persecution and suffering has become the cornerstone of a civilization and of nations whose very position in modern life has too often been secured by ruthless use of power applied to weak and defenseless peoples....The masses of (people) live with their back constantly against the wall. They are the poor, the disinherited, the dispossessed. What does our religion say to them?[16]

Our response to this dehumanization challenge must be guided by the particular with simultaneous confrontation of the universal through the ubiquitous and unlimited power of the Holy

---

14 Ronald E. Peters, *Urban Ministry: An Introduction,* 58.

15 Peters, 58.

16 Howard Thurman, *Jesus and the Disinherited,* 11.

Spirit. The particulars (the place) are the individual challenges such as homelessness, economic discrimination, unequal justice, dysfunctional family structures, physical and psychological abuse, drug abuse, irrelevant or partial counseling, disproportionate unemployment, inadequate public school education, etc. The universals (the space) are the systemic oppressive structures that perpetuate, by any means necessary, the chronic existence of the particular challenges, often resulting in an outcome of serving time in prison for the economically- and ethnically-oppressed.

In the context of the new city, the church must overcome these psycho-spiritual obstacles and press forward to heal the scars of oppressive dehumanization, by understanding that there must be a mutual relationship between the oppressed and the oppressor that overcomes dehumanization or, as defined by Paolo Freire, the "banking" concept of education." According to Freire, there is a banking model of education that turns students into "receptacles" to be "filled" by the teachers, like making deposits at a bank. The teacher deposits and students are the depositories. Students receive, memorize, and repeat.[17] And since we "receive" the world as passive entities, this type of education makes us more passive still, attuning us to our world so that we do not question it.

The banking model tries to control thinking and action and inhibits creative powers, thus self-imposing spiritual incarceration and ministerial isolation. It is fighting and struggling through learned insecurity and fear just beneath the surface, to maintain the submersion of consciousness. To not acknowledge this paradigm of banking education relinquishes the power inherent inside every Christian made by God with an *imago dei* expectation, to become complacent spectators, seeking to achieve tasks and checklists rather than sustainable spirit-filled results.[18] Conversely in Freire's problem-posing education concept:

> The educator chooses to constantly re-form his reflections in the reflections of the students who

---

17 Paulo Freire, *Pedagogy of the Oppressed,* 58.

18 Ibid.

are now critical co-investigators in dialogue with the teacher, thus moving toward mutual humanization. The concept of problem-posing education involves a constant unveiling of reality, the emergence of consciousness, and critical intervention in reality.[19]

Problem-posing education is the practice of freedom rather than the practice of domination. In the case of the church and the city, the initial oppressors responsible for the scars in many cases no longer exist but have passed away, leaving a remnant of shackled confidence in the hearts and minds of those still struggling with unrealized and deep-seated psycho-spiritual strongholds. And so the church, in collaboration with all stakeholders of the city, must now go forth through the method of problem-posing education to integrate the virtual and physical remnant of the oppressor in the mutual healing and deliverance process.

Although oppression dehumanizes both or all parties and stifles their humanity, according to Freire in order for there to be sustainable change, the oppressed must lead the struggle for a fuller humanity for both. "The oppressor, who is himself dehumanized because he dehumanizes others, tries to hang onto his power and dehumanizing practices."[20] "When the oppressed seeks to regain and deepen their humanity, they must not in turn oppress the oppressors, but rather help to restore the humanity of both."[21] The contradiction between the two classes is resolved by the appearance of a new kind of human being, one in the process of liberation. It is not possible to eliminate oppression just by a shift of roles in which the oppressor becomes the oppressed and vice-versa.[22] "In such change we can't say that one person liberates himself, or another, but that people in collaborative communion liberate each other."[23]

---

19 Ibid., 68.

20 Freire, 32.

21 Ibid., 28.

22 Ibid., 42.

23 Ibid., 128.

Oppression in the new city is a symptom of secularization, but not only of the city. It is more a derivative symptom caused from secularization of the infiltrated and therefore lethargic temple or church. Secularization of the city bolsters anonymity of sin, because quite often "community" in the 21st century city operates through a virtual filter, a filter that takes precedence over face-to-face communication and relationships.[24] This secularization of the city is subtle, for it quietly manipulates "deliverance from metaphysical and religious control over humanity's reason and language."[25]

In response, the temple must be ubiquitous and without moral compromise; for it must be separate and simultaneously relevant at the center of the secularization of the city. For some, secularization is the process of removing the "religious tutelage" from our society so that liberation can occur.[26] But the liberation to which they refer is psychological and physical and without consideration for the eternal liberation and freedom of soul salvation that only the church can provide through connection with Jesus Christ. The church cannot be so separate from this secularization that it is no longer relevant; the church must remain the church, the tent of meeting, the God-saturated temple in the midst of the wilderness, in the midst of the darkness, in the midst of the manger and in the midst of the storm.

The starting point today for any theology of the church must be a theology of the cross; it must be a theology of social change (transformation, reconciliation, and restoration). According to Harvey Cox,

> The church must dislodge itself from "static theology," retrospective thinking and action and work to be fully awake, alert and active – shaped by what God is

---

24 Quentine J. Schultz, *Symbolic Ambiguity – Limitations of Human Communication: Communicating for Life - Christian Stewardship in Community and Media Communicating for Life*, 71.

25 Harvey Cox, *The Secular City*, i.

26 Ibid., 18.

now doing in the world. In this way, the church is in partnership with the Divine Master of Redevelopment in constructing and re-forming a theology of revolution and of politics that leads to a more comprehensive theology of revolutionary social change.[27]

The church must set itself high upon a hill that cannot be hidden, for there are times when the church will be sacrificially on a hill outside of the physical city, but more importantly it must always remain spiritually inside, at the center of the city. Whether the church is bruised, beaten, tired and stretched wide on that hill, surrounded on one side by last-minute supporters and on the other by hatred and pessimism, the church must remain steadfast in the center on that cross, embracing sacrifice for all the inhabitants of the new city.

As fiercely as those who crucified Jesus on the cross, capitalism has become the new religion in the new city that gives birth to secularization, religious reorganization, religious individualization and supply-side methods that compromise the moral viability of the church and therefore the city. Ultimately, capitalism is an economic system in which the means of production are privately-owned and controlled, characterized by relentless and uncompromising competition with a motive of achieving power, financial leadership, and profit. The derivative impact of living reactively or strictly according to capitalistic expectations is in contrast to Romans Chapter 8.

> [5] For those who live according to the flesh set their minds on the things of the flesh, but those that live according to the Spirit, the things of the Spirit. [6] For to be carnally minded is death, but to be spiritually minded is life and peace.

Based on this premise, economics and capitalism have competed with, morphed, infiltrated and overshadowed the church

---

27 Ibid., 91.

to the point of systematic secularization of the family structure, all culture, and political power throughout society and the city. Prioritization on prosperous industrial complexes has dominated those things that were once sacred, including the church. This secular emphasis has created a society of moral "haves" and "have-nots," as the church is diluted by economic distraction both in terms of message and implementation. The church has become more focused on numbers and revenue than being the tough-loving, moral compass of society. The silencing of the prophetic voice that once called out and took action against social ills has become the stealth weapon of mass destruction that has forgotten about its mandate to relentlessly save those few sheep that may seek to become the digitally-powered and desensitized annihilator of the current day. Where is the prophetic voice? Where is the prophetic action at the center of the new city that must come from the church?

In Plato's *Republic*, Plato asserts that wealth tends to corrupt and distract individuals from their true purpose. Plato emphasizes the need for justice as a measure for a healthy city starting with the just man, and that the just man should be measured to be just by the faculty of the individual soul.[28] For Plato, a just man does not differ from a just city; he felt that justice itself is not the exclusive responsibility of any one class of citizens, but emerges from the harmonious relationship of each component of the society with every other.[29] But Plato also posits that a person does not owe full and absolute loyalty to any earthly society. Based on Christian doctrine, Saint Augustine examined this last statement of Plato. He felt that *sola scriptura* instructed human beings about the highest good and the highest evil and without such guidance, humans have no purpose. Augustine went on to focus this argument in the *City of God* where he categorized and established the areas of participation and choice for each soul to include the church, the state, the city of heaven, and the city of the world. For Augustine, the church was divinely-created and established to lead human-

---

28 G.M.A. Grube, *Plato Republic*, 119.

29 Marcus Dods, *The City of God: Saint: Augustine*, 773.

kind to soul salvation and eternal goodness, which is God. Ideally, the state adheres to the virtues of politics and logic, formulating a political community. Both societies, the church and the state, are visible to humankind and both seek to do good for humankind. Simultaneously mirroring these two invisible societies of church and state are the city of heaven, for those predestined for salvation, and the city of the world, for those given eternal damnation. Augustine felt that upon knowledge, humankind must pursue the city of heaven to maintain a proper sense of order and peace. His thesis in the *City of God* is a challenge to humankind to choose of which city it wishes to be a part. Augustine sees his role and the role of the church as clearly defining the parameters, choices or consequences necessary for inclusion in each simultaneously-invisible alternative or city. Augustine concludes that the purpose of time and existence is to show through the church the magnification of God's plan, which involves fostering the City of Heaven and saturating it with worthy inhabitants.

But the church now sits, more than forty-five years after the passing of the Civil Rights legislation that allowed African Americans to vote, in a seemingly passive position. One can rightly ask: and what has been done with any lasting perseverance to reconcile and restore God's people? People like those slaves generations removed from the 50 million slaughtered souls of the holocaust of the middle passage, those who persevered to survive through the unimaginable, the ones who owned nothing but their faith and trust and their willingness to be used to do God's will, what about their perseverance? People like the ones who did not surrender to their earthly circumstance, yet relinquished everything for absolute obedience and dependence on God's will for themselves and those around them. People like those slaves who, after their masters went to sleep, sneaked out into the hush harbors in the woods, waiting in collective prayer for the proclamation and reality of an unknown and unpredictable freedom, yet still trusting God. What about their perseverance and where are those who continue their tradition of pursuing justice and restoration?

In so many ways today, in 2012, we the "dream deferred" – the black, the white, the yellow, the brown, and the red – sit and stand at the end of a sacrificial and bloody 400 years, silently allowing the reproduction of a corporate chattel slavery through the prison-industrial complex, satisfied with feel-good charity ministry that does little to change the systemic issues or to holistically transform the individuals impacted negatively by the current criminal justice system and other social illnesses due to economic oppression of the least of these in society. We must ask ourselves the questions, for how bold will we be to establish a prophetic platform that addresses both the systemic universal and the hemorrhaging particular? Are we the church, or is there another?

The congregants who must cry out from the wilderness to become the restoration agents who will make the crooked places straight, the valleys exalted, and the mountains attainable are the pastors, the community activists, the Body of Christ and the economically and spiritually disinherited.[30] Restoration must be initiated by the oppressed with inclusion of all stakeholders, through the establishment of a global digital ministry platform (internet, desktop, laptop, smart-phone, etc.) that is collaborative, multi-lingual and accessible to individuals with disabilities, while enhancing the collective church's gifts and resources and with the ability to provide holistic counseling/pastoral care, sharing of best practices, discipleship, and the ability to organize community action against injustice. This platform will seek to erase the digital/energy divide for the deeply-impoverished by allowing people in collaborative communion to liberate each other through loving sacrifice and daily praxis.[31]

The foundation for the theology of the digital ministry platform must be centered on radical discipleship.[32] The church and the

30 C.K. Prahald, *The Fortune at the Bottom of the Pyramid: Eradicating Poverty through Profits*, 6.

31 Jesse Rice, *The Church of Facebook: How the Hyperconnected are Redefining Community*, 187.

32 Schultz, 137.

platform must be willing to stay on the cross, as the foundation for proclamation and action, in order to save souls who are given the knowledge to make a choice between the city of heaven and the city of the world. Those yet un-awakened souls must be given scripture that will fortify their willingness to stand at the foot of the cross to carry their brothers and sisters, and to know though they may feel exhausted, beaten down, overwhelmed and far away from God at times; if they are willing to sacrifice in love for God in the flesh, they will remain closest to God in the spirit. For through this medium the church must speak to those whose backs are half-turned between God and capitalism and salvation; it must show compassion to those who lament to God with an expectation of deliverance because they know and understand that God is well able to overcome it. The church must stand at the center of the moral divide in the new city to transform, renew, and restore the minds of its inhabitants.

Ultimately the challenge to the church is to overcome a dehumanizing neo-colonialism that is powered by a stealthy and destructive digital secularization; for the church must now be witness and passionately offer a transformative and restorative theology of social change. Through the ministry of pre-emptive presence, the church must wrestle with the economic aspects of socially-networked life, not as a distraction but as a vehicle through which power and resources are brought to bear on the spiritual and material aspects of life in the city. It is through such sacrifice and submission starting with the church, that the digitally "connected city" as new creation will serve as the instrument through which God will transform and redeem an urbanizing world.

CHAPTER TWO
Digital Secularization

The definition of neo-colonialism initially established in 1965 by Kwame Nkrumah, the first post-independence President of Ghana, has been discussed by a number of twentieth century scholars and is the practice of using capitalism, globalization, and cultural forces to control a country or a collective in lieu of direct military or political control. Such control may be economic, cultural or linguistic; by promoting one's own culture, language or media, so that embedded corporations and organizations in that culture can make better headway in opening and monopolizing markets in those countries. And so, neo-colonialism within Nkrumah's definition would be the end result of relatively benign business interests leading to deleterious cultural effects.[33]

In the 21st century, neo-colonialism has silently integrated and systematically evolved to control all aspects of collective thought including commerce, government and entire cultures through a radical technology driven digital secularization that is capable of impacting both developing countries and global superpowers. Secularization is manifested as an evil or unholy cause in the desacralized and diminished consciousness of cruel inhumanity and gross indignities to people globally, leaving a trail of broken lives, relationships and broken spirits. This digital form of secularization is the ubiquitous expansion of secularization through the integrated use of technology within social processes that interpret and measure the interaction of religious world-views and practices with other aspects of social life. Digital Secularization is therefore the immoral use of

---

33 Kwame Nkrumah, *Neo-Colonialism, the Last Stage of Imperialism*, Introduction. http://www.marxists.org/subject/africa/nkrumah/neo-colonialism/

technology for greedy exploitation of people. It is my opinion that the reinforcement of neo-colonialism through digital secularization will result in a desacralization of the world, transposition of religious institutions and disengagement of society from virtually any form of morality, more particularly as pertains to religion. It is my assertion that in 2012, through the digital secularization of prison-industrial complexes, military-industrial complexes, governments, economies, education and mass media, health, energy and natural resources, religion, and technology, neo-colonialism has caused an increased divide between the few that control global wealth and the many that are controlled by a dehumanizing poverty.

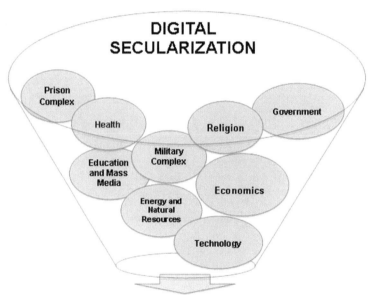

This dehumanizing poverty can no longer be ignored. As of August 2011, unemployment in the United States was at 9.1% with the African American unemployment rate increasing to 16.7% and the white unemployment rate falling slightly to 8%.[34]

---

34 Annalyn Censky, *Black Unemployment: Highest in 27 years*, September 2, 2011. CNN Money. http://money.cnn.com/2011/09/02/news/economy/black_unemployment_rate/ [accessed September 5, 2011]

The effects of the recession of 2008 have pushed more of God's children (independent of ethnicity) into unfathomable financial situations, poverty and, in some cases, homelessness. The overwhelming indicator with respect to homelessness is the continuing rise in deep poverty, which increased to a record level of 20.5 million people in 2010. This marked the fourth consecutive annual increase in deep poverty and raised the deep poverty rate to 6.7 percent.[35]

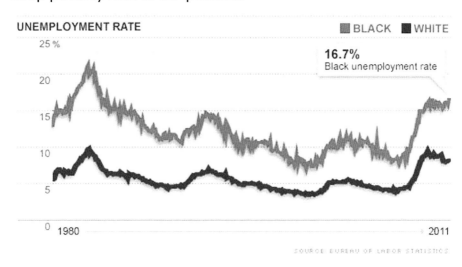

UNEMPLOYMENT RATE   ■ BLACK ■ WHITE

16.7%
Black unemployment rate

1980   2011

SOURCE: BUREAU OF LABOR STATISTICS

In contrast, in 2009 banks, securities firms, and insurance companies lowered their combined losses from a staggering $213 billion to just $20 billion. Buoyed by a government bailout, AIG (AIG, Fortune 500) swung from a loss of $99 billion in 2008 (a Fortune 500 record) to a deficit of $11 billion last year. The banks and brokers, including J.P. Morgan (JPM, Fortune 500), Wells Fargo (WFC, Fortune 500), and Goldman Sachs (GS, Fortune 500), rebounded from losses of $8.7 billion in 2008 to $38 billion in profits in 2009.[36]

---

35 National Alliance to End Homelessness. *Increases in Homelessness on the Horizon*, September 28, 2011. http://www.endhomelessness.org/content/article/detail/4226 [accessed October 15, 2011]

36 Fortune 500, September 15, 2011. http://money.cnn.com/magazines/fortune/fortune500/2009/snapshots/2608.html?source=story_f500_link [accessed October 15, 2011]

In the midst of the rebounds on Wall Street and the many economic challenges on the horizon, the most vulnerable populations (the least of these) have been hit the hardest. The average income for working poor people decreased more than 2 percent between late 2010 and 2011. Nearly 6 million poor households are now severely housing-cost burdened, meaning about 3 out of every 4 poor households pay more than 50 percent of income on rent. The number of people in poverty has increased to a record 46.2 million and the poverty rate of 15.1 percent is the highest on record since 1983.[37]

In 2005, 25.7 million Americans needed food stamps; in 2011, 45.8 million people relied on them to eat.[38] And Congress is considering cutting the funding for the food stamp program, this at a time when the *Department of Agriculture* estimates that an additional 22.5 million people will need them, bringing the total number of Americans in need of food assistance to a staggering 68.3 million people by 2012.[39] Has the influence of neo-colonialism caused the church to question its God-given power to take a few loaves of bread and a couple of fish and feed thousands? Or to attempt to take a jar of oil and a cup of flour to consistently and reliably feed a few? Where is the church on this sin of domestic and global poverty and hunger, for poverty and hunger are moral issues where the church must be relentless, central and present. As the chart below shows, the time for the church is now, for the number of people in need of food stamps has been rapidly increasing year-after-year.[40]

37 *Income, Poverty, and Health Insurance Coverage in the United States:2009*, U.S. Census.gov, http://www.census.gov/prod/2010pubs/p60-238.pdf [accessed October 15, 2011]

38 Dottie Rosenbaum, *The Food Stamp Program is Growing to Meet Need*. Center on Budget and Policy Priorities, July 12, 2006. http://www.cbpp.org/cms/index.cfm?fa=view&id=460 [accessed October 15, 2011]

39 United Press International, *House Wants to Cut Food Stamps*, http://www.arcamax.com/health/healthtips/s-917916-690577 [accessed October 15, 2011]

40 USDA – Supplemental Nutrition Assistance Program (SNAP): *Number of Persons Participating Nationally/by State* http://www.fns.usda.gov/pd/29SNAPcurrPP.htm [accessed October 15, 2011]

U.S. Food Stamp Participation

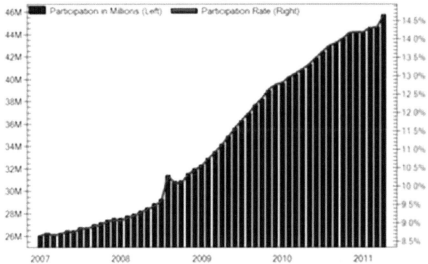

Source SNAP

The number of U.S. homes receiving foreclosure filings will climb about 20 percent in 2011, reaching a peak for the housing crisis, as unemployment remains high and banks resume seizures as a result of the economic slowdown. A record 2.87 million properties, received notices of repossession or default auction in 2010, a 2 percent increase from a year earlier. Banks seized more than 1 million homes in 2010, up 14 percent from a year earlier. About 3 million homes have been repossessed since the housing boom ended in 2006, and according to experts, this number could balloon to about 6 million by 2013, when the housing market may absorb the bulk of distressed properties.[41]

This dehumanizing poverty is systemic; through the acts of organizations such as the American Legislative Exchange Council (ALEC) and other organizations, poverty has essentially become

---

41 Dan Levy and Prashant Gopal, *Foreclosure Filings in U.S. May Jump 20% From Record 2010 as Crisis Peaks*, January 13, 2011, Bloomberg. http://www.bloomberg.com/news/2011-01-13/u-s-foreclosure-filings-may-jump-20-this-year-as-crisis-peaks.html [accessed November 09, 2011]

a crime. In 2008 there was $17 billion cut from public housing programs, while there was an increase of $19 billion in programs for building prisons, "effectively making the construction of prisons the nation's main housing program for the poor."[42]

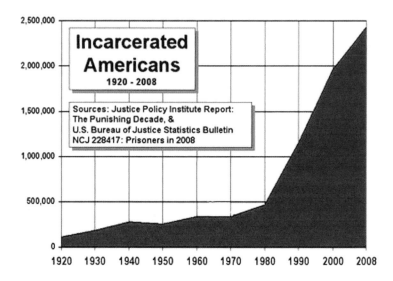

Before laws began to be rewritten in 1980, with direct input from ALEC, there was a prison population in the United States of 500,000 citizens. After laws were rewritten to target poor inner city citizens with much more severe penalties, the US prison population has skyrocketed to 2.4 million people. With only 4% of the world's population, we have 25% of the world's prison population, the largest prison population in the world.

In 2000, Columbia University's School of Public Health conducted an intensive examination of mortality and medical data and estimated that 875,000 deaths were attributed to a cluster of social factors bound up with poverty and income inequality.[43]

---

42 David Cole, *Can Our Shameful Prisons Be Reformed*. http://www.nybooks. com/articles/archives/2009/nov/19/can-our-shameful-prisons-be-reformed/ [accessed November 09, 2011]

43 Debra Watson, *The Dramatic Effect of Poverty on Death Rates in the US*, http:// www.wsws.org/articles/2011/jul2011/pove-j13.shtml [accessed November 09, 2011]

This means that 1 out of every 35.5 people living in poverty die *annually* as a result of their impoverishment. Extrapolation of this data to the 2009 total of 52.8 million people living in poverty shows an estimate of 1,486,338 deaths within that year. Even if you use the lower poverty totals from the Census Bureau, 43.6 million people, you get an estimate of 1,228,169 deaths in 2009.

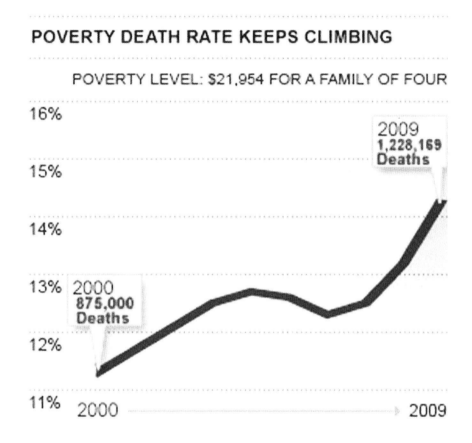

POVERTY DEATH RATE KEEPS CLIMBING

POVERTY LEVEL: $21,954 FOR A FAMILY OF FOUR

Many of the aforementioned economic indicators are forecast to remain bleak in the near future, according to sources as varied as the Congressional Budget Office (CBO), the Office of Budget and Management (OMB), and the Economist Intelligence Unit (EIU), a leading private sector research and analysis firm. For example, in response to new data on GDP growth, investment markets, unemployment, and other economic health indicators, both the CBO and OMB in their respective economic outlook reports have revised their forecasts to reflect the worsening economic conditions across the country. The expectation is that the United States will continue to see poor economic conditions for years to come with, for example, the unemployment rate projected to hover near 9 percent until 2013 and then not reach pre-2007 to 2009 recession levels until 2016 or 2017. These continuing poor economic conditions likely mean high levels of poverty and deep poverty will remain. In fact, the Brookings Institution projects poverty will continue to increase through 2012 and that the poverty rate will stay above 15 percent through 2014. The Brookings' research predicts poverty will stay above pre-2007 to 2009 recession levels through 2020. Deep poverty follows a similar trajectory, so it is predicted that the deep poverty rate will remain at levels not seen since before the current economic downturn starting in 2008.[44]

The issue of dehumanizing poverty is not only a United States problem it is a global crisis, for World Bank figures for world poverty reveals a higher number of people living in poverty than previously thought. For example, the new poverty line is defined as living on the equivalent of $1.25 a day. With that measure based on latest data available (2005), 1.4 billion people live on or below that line. Furthermore, almost half the world, over three billion people, live on less than $2.50 a day and at least 80% of humanity lives on less than $10 a day.[45]

If poverty is the result of a dehumanization that is the symptomatic success of neo-colonialism at this point in human progress and creation, how can the church stand knee-deep in the innocent blood of our brothers and sisters, inactively watching that which is antithetical to God? For dehumanization is to relegate, demean and treat another human being as if he or she were

44 National Alliance to End Homelessness. *Increases in Homelessness on the Horizon*, September 28, 2011. http://www.endhomelessness.org/content/article/detail/4226 [accessed October 15, 2011]

45 Poverty Facts and Stats, http://www.globalissues.org/article/26/poverty-facts-and-stats [accessed November 09, 2011]

less than human, not a member of the family of humankind. It is time for the church to take a sanctified stand against neo-colonialism. This neo-colonialism through global digital secularization competes with the compassion, sacrifice and morality of the church in order to rationalize and reinforce apathetic behaviors such as oppression, persecution and exploitation, thus achieving capitalism by any means necessary.

The secularization to which I refer has penetrated the conscience of society, reaching deep down past our spiritual ethic to anesthetize or paralyze the subconscious through methods of religious individualization, religious reorganization, and a supply-side infiltration, thus diluting that which was once sacred and holy. In 2011 secularization in its current form redacts the morality of religion from society, while simultaneously limiting religious morality back into society to come primarily from those religious institutions that have been compromised by secularization. This dynamic is reinforced through a digital form of secularization that now moves and adapts at the speed of thought, thus attempting to silence the transforming and restorative voice and power of the church.

An extensive survey from May through August 2007 by the Pew Forum on Religion & Public Life details statistics that reveal more than one-quarter of American adults (28%) have left the faith in which they were raised in favor of another religion, or no religion at all. If change in affiliation from one type of Protestantism to another is included, 44% of adults have either switched religious affiliation, moved from being unaffiliated with any religion to being affiliated with a particular faith, or dropped altogether any connection to a specific religious tradition. The survey also finds that the number of people who say they are unaffiliated with any particular faith today (16.1%) is more than double the number who say they were not affiliated with any particular religion as children. Among Americans ages 18-29, one in four say they are not currently affiliated with any particular religion. The Landscape Survey confirms that the United States is on the verge of becoming a minority Protestant country; the number of Americans who report that they are members of Protestant denominations now stands at barely 51%.[46] These results are a reflection of the increased secularization of the church, for the church has morphed from a primary mindset of saving souls to an assimilated secular supply-side mindset of competing to win souls in the "religious market place." The challenge of succumbing to a supply- side mindset is the establishment of a competitive and systemic division within the church itself, thus rendering the collaborative gifts of the overall church fractured and paralyzed by earthly aspiration and economic achievement rather than spiritual fruit.

In *The Secular City*, Harvey Cox interprets the aforementioned digital secularization to be a technopolis. A technopolis represents a technical foundation upon which the secular city rests and from which the polis summons up the social and cultural institutions and systems resident within a newly-formed urban civilization, or what was previously referred to in Chapter 1 as " the new city." According to Cox, it is within the tension or catalytic gap of this technopolis that social change occurs. The current catalytic gap that exists between the polis of the political and the technical points to the need for humanity and the church to act in response to the need for transformation, compassion, morality and ultimately reconciliation of souls.[47] From a biblical standpoint, "the catalytic gap exists within the semicolon of the Mark text: 'The time is fulfilled and the Kingdom of God is at hand; repent and believe the Gospel.'" This is the "already, but not yet" interpreted for us in the phrase "in the process of becoming." In this way we understand that the promise is in the press toward the mark, because for now, we know in part, but on the other side of the eschaton we will know perfection completely.

And so as the church moves to be central and present in the midst of dehumanization, poverty and digital secularization, it must do so with sight for the institutional differentiation that is

---

46 The Pew Forum on Religion and Public Life: *U.S. Religious Landscape Survey* http://religions.pewforum.org/reports [accessed November 09, 2011]

47 Cox, 100.

now resident. For today the poor box has been replaced by the welfare office, the pastoral counselor by the psychologist, and the religious order's hospice by the hospital corporation.[48] There is now a societalization in the church and the surrounding community; for almost everywhere in the modern world, small-scale communities have lost power to large-scale organizations: huge corporations, mass media, marketing, and political bureaucracies. The church must acknowledge that religion has become tied up with the life of the local community, suffering the same moral erosion; for the role of religion in public life has been relegated to a privatization that has caused a significant decline in religious belief. This decline in belief is also a symptom of pluralism, for pluralism acts as secular peer pressure causing those who might believe to assimilate and coexist with beliefs that are based on a "worldly" view. There is also the challenge of rationalization, such as rational science, rational business organizations, and rational laws, all of which compete directly with the mission and mindset of the church.[49]

And so in the midst of the many challenges faced by the church, how might the church use evolving religious reorganization in the United States and globally as a platform for confronting secularization, and move toward a theology of social change? While religious reorganization provides intimacy in terms of the particular needs of smaller congregations, the church must remain thoughtful and obedient to press toward God's charge of collaborative global restoration and reconciliation. When the church is not stretching and pressing as ambassadors of reconciliation seeking to find the un-awakened and lost sheep, there is growth in religious individualization where individuals conveniently pull from multiple religions to create their own convenient beliefs in the name of spirituality, which undercuts the ethos of the church and religion itself. Upon analysis of the aforementioned, it is clear that both the church and the world are in the midst of a digital paradigm change.

---

48 Meredith B. McGuire, *Religion: The Social Context*, 286.

49 Ibid., 287.

Hans Küng applied the concept of paradigm change to the history of Christian thought. He cited five major historical paradigms: Greek Alexandrian, Latin Augustinian, Medieval Thomistic, Reformation and Modern Critical. Each Paradigm provided a framework for normal work and cumulative growth in which the scope of the paradigm was extended and major change was resisted. Küng argued that each new paradigm arose in a period of crisis and uncertainty. He used the challenges of Gnosticism in the Hellenistic world, and the rise of science and biblical criticism in the 20th century as examples.[50] Each new paradigm arose from a fresh experience of the original message of Jesus Christ, as well as institutional crisis and external challenges. In a similar vein to Küng, Stephan Pfürtner suggested that it follows that we must then consider Luther's idea of justification by faith as a new paradigm, for it led to the reconstruction of prior beliefs and the reinterpretation of previous data in a new framework of thought.[51] The church is now faced with the global paradigm of neo-colonialism and digital secularization; and if the church is willing to boldly respond through a theology of social change, there will be transformation to a spiritual paradigm of collaborative digital restoration.

But how will the church react to the change in paradigm while pro-actively and pre-emptively establishing a theology of social change? A theology of social change must first establish why immediate action is necessary in order to catalyze the church. It must identify the reasons for inaction and then analyze the cause for inactivity. A strategy must be established to bring the people out of a political paralysis that eradicates the roots of inaction. And finally there must be 'a social denouement' which turns things upside down and inside out, that shocks the unconscious into purposeful social action.[52] There must be a *metanoia*, a radical change where the scales fall from the eyes, a new conscious-

---

50 Ian G. Barbour, *Religion and Science: Historical and Contemporary Issues, Models and Paradigms*, 129.

51 Barbour, 130.

52 Cox, 99.

ness emerges and all things are made new. While secularization both precedes and follows urbanization, God must be a part of both, leading us through the process of conversion that leads to responsibility and accountability in order to actualize a theology of social change. And through a theology of social change the church, like Jesus, must now reconcile by functioning as cultural exorcist.

A theology of social change was the four-step, non-violent approach taken during the Montgomery bus boycott led by Rev. Dr. Martin Luther King, Jr. The four-step method included (not in any specific linear order) collection of the facts to determine whether injustices are alive; negotiation of modified circumstances that lead all parties to a place of sustainable healing and reconciliation; continuous self-purification and discipleship; and direct non-violent action whenever applicable.[53] A theology of social change was reflected through the action of the nuns who were associated with Mother Theresa, the ones who lived in AIDS hospices in Manhattan in the early 1980s. These were nuns who fearlessly loved and cleaned the blood- and pus-filled wounds of those left behind dying of AIDS, at a time when society was terrified more by the possibility of contamination than the possibility of sacrificial reconciliation. A theology of social change was the Amish community in Nickel Mines, PA, in 2006 that personally lost so much in the senseless murder of loved ones including young children, yet forgave the gunman and extended sincere tender compassion and concern to the gunman's family.

A theology of social change is not easy, for it requires the strength and perseverance to break through the digital tomb of despair facing the church. According to Webster's Dictionary a tomb is a repository for the remains of the dead. In earlier days it was virtually always a chamber excavated from fortified rock, specifically for receiving human remains. But how long will the "dead in spirit" remain incarcerated in a tomb? How long will we, the striving remnant, those seeking eternal life, be confined to a

---

53 Martin Luther King, Jr., *The Essential Writings and Speeches of Martin Luther King, Jr.,* 290.

spiritual tomb? How long will it be before we, the church, begin to take down strongholds, once and for all, to boldly overcome the oppression of our spirit by our flesh?

For when they betrayed Jesus and beat Him, and dragged Him through the streets, and spit on Him and called Him names, because He was the Word that was there in the beginning with God, the One who had come to save the world, His disposition could not be controlled by the impending and sure reality of a tomb. And so He said, "Father, forgive them, for they do not know what they do."

Because He was there in the garden in the beginning during the Edenic Covenant in the Old Testament, finally on the Cross when the soldiers divided His garments and pressed thorns in His skull, and cast lots for his belongings, He would not be confined to a tomb of bitterness. He said, "Father, forgive them, for they do not know what they do."

Because He was there in the beginning during the Adamic, Noahic, Abrahamic, and Mosaic Covenants in the Old Testament, on the Cross when the thief asked to be removed from the tomb of un-forgiveness, rather than eternal condemnation, Jesus said to him, "Assuredly, I say to you, today you will be with Me in Paradise."

Because He was there during the Palestinian, Davidic and New covenants where He wrote love upon our hearts, while on the cross, in excruciating pain, when Jesus therefore saw His mother, and the disciple John, whom He loved standing by; He said to His mother, "Woman, behold your son!" Then He said to the disciple, "Behold your mother!" And from that hour, that disciple took her to his own *home.* **"In** that moment Jesus showed those who are willing to stand and trust Him, that neither death nor life, nor angel nor principality, nor power, nor things present nor things to come, nor height nor depth nor any other created thing shall ever separate them from His love. In that moment He showed us that God's love, no matter the trial or the circumstance, never fails.

And because He was there with the Children of Israel through-out their disobedience and wilderness experiences, to witness and receive their burnt offerings, and grain offerings, and meal offerings, and fellowship offerings, and peace offerings, and sin offerings, and trespass offerings, He was well within His divinity after that ninth hour of relentless torture when He cried out with a loud voice, saying, "Eli, Eli, lama sabachthani?" that is, *"My God, my God why hast Thou forsaken Me?"*

And after turning water into wine as a symbolic representation of His power to make real in the world His ability to convert one thing to another thing, one circumstance to another circumstance, in the blink of an eye; after witnessing to the woman at the well; after showing equality by witnessing to the Samaritans for whom Jews had no dealings; after healing the nobleman's son; after saving the soul of a paralytic and then healing his body; not because of the faith of the paralytic but because of the faith of the four men who were willing to humble themselves in order to carry their friend up and through the roof; after manifesting the Holy Spirit that indwelled within Him to feed 5,000 souls with only five loaves of bread and a few fish; after teaching the disciples by walking on water, so that they too would walk on water if that is what they were required to do; after yearning through the abrasive rejection of so many potential followers whose sins He could have washed away; after advocating and saving a woman who was caught in adultery, by making a simple statement "let him who is without sin cast the first stone;" after giving a blind man sight, raising Lazarus from the dead, being pierced in His side, saying "I thirst," and then being given sour wine, and finally proclaiming that it is finished, Jesus cried out with a loud voice, saying, "Father, *'into Your hands I commit My spirit.'*" And having said this, He breathed His last.

In that very moment, in that last breath, when death looked final, with all of the offerings and sacrifices of the Old Testament combined; Jesus, the Incarnate Word of God made flesh, relinquished the divine power of the Holy Spirit to give the ultimate sacrifice, to absorb every tomb and every sin for all humankind forever, if we believe. At that awesome, amazing, wonder-working moment, the blueprint and foundation for a theology of social change was established and handed to us all for every circumstance throughout all changing times.

CHAPTER THREE

I-Generation Transformation

In a December 17, 2011, Associated Press article, Sheldon Danziger, a University of Michigan public policy professor who specializes in poverty stated, "According to the U.S. Census Bureau, 1 in 2 persons in the United States has fallen into poverty or is now scraping by on earnings that classify them as low income."[54] While the church faces universal challenges such as neo-colonialism, digital secularization, political uprisings, growing atheism, racism, and a vast increase in domestic and global poverty, it must do so with fervent love and primary consideration for the particular soul of the individual. If the church is to be the collective agent of social change it must act out its theology with resolute compassion not only for the dispossessed, the disenfranchised and the disinherited, but equally for those who cause such dehumanization. As Lee Butler, the professor of pastoral care and theology warns us, the church must be prepared to wrestle with the protracted traumatic stress felt by individuals from the aforementioned challenges.[55]

Simply put, the church must be willing to sift through modern conflict, digital manipulation, and economic limitations by boldly preaching and acting upon the uncompromised Gospel of Jesus Christ to the boardrooms, the city halls, the state capitols and Capitol Hill, and to all of the secularized theological organizations, and those affected by them. As Mary and Joseph traveled toward the unknown, carrying the hope, redemption and salvation of the

---

54 http:// http://www.census.gov/prod/2011pubs/p60-239.pdf (accessed October 12, 2011)

55 Lee. H. Butler, Jr., *Liberating our Dignity, Saving our Souls*, 161.

world in Jesus Christ to be born in a lowly dark and filthy manger; the church must now move by faith and not by sight to the center of global urbanization (the new internet city) carrying transformation, restoration and reconciliation to the many souls oppressed by unwarranted earthly circumstance.

With an exponential attack on morality through technology and digital secularization, the church can no longer be satisfied with status quo protests. The church must be the catalyst for revolutionary yet peaceful confrontation, transformation, uncompromised restoration and social change. According to James H. Cone in his book *Black Theology and Black Power*,

> Revolution sees every particular wrong as one more instance in a pattern which is itself beyond rectification. Revolution aims at the substitution of a new system for one adjudged to be corrupt, rather than corrective adjustments within the existing system; the power of revolution is coercive.[56]

Revolution must cause corrective change to both the systemic and the particular aspects of an existence or circumstance. The revolution that the church inspires, and shares collaborative leadership must be a radical ministry platform that is focused on the mind, heart and soul of the individual (both the haves and the have-nots). Romans 12:1-2 states,

> [1] I beseech you therefore, brethren, by the mercies of God, that you present your bodies a living sacrifice, holy, acceptable to God, which is your reasonable service. [2] And do not be conformed to this world, but be transformed by the renewing of your mind, that you may prove what *is* that good and acceptable and perfect will of God.

---

56 James H. Cone, *Black Theology and Black Power,* 136.

The church must now yield to a collaborative revolution, one that invokes psycho-spiritual infiltration based on the ethic of the Gospel throughout cyberspace. This involves both the body and the mind, since that which is conceived in the mind is carried out in the body; thus one's whole being must be presented by a decisive act of the will of God for His service. As Jesus did, the church must yield to do: whatever and however God commands.

Yielding will lead not only to dedication but also to separation: "do not be conformed to this world." Since the world is resolutely opposed to God, we cannot revel in its lusts and at the same time do the will of God. The church must remain separate while being central and present in the midst of sin. The concept of separation means being unfashionable in spirit, thought, values, and actions, according to the world's standards. Yielding includes transformation of the mind, which is sanctified through a lifetime of renewing the mind.

But with technology and global urbanization, renewal of the mind is under relentless attack, attempts to darken the mind with sin are constant, so the mind must be brought to a place where it thinks as God thinks. Renewal of the mind must encompass an awakening to the many causal factors that stimulate behavior, prayers to God in every circumstance, and constant meditation on the word of God.

Quite often the causal factors specific to deviant behavior are the result of stress or stimuli causing the type of reaction that is antithetical to the church and God's creation.[57] Causal factors flow throughout the cycle of abuse both for the oppressed and the oppressor, and this can lead to an unfortunate cycle of recidivism, where there is a reengagement by the oppressed back toward the responsible oppressive stimuli due to hopelessness, fear and familiarity.[58] The causal factors also include protracted-traumatic stress, which is different than post-traumatic stress. Post-traumatic stress is based on the idea that a trauma was a one-time event in the past that continues to traumatize the

---

57 Coleman, Butcher, Carson, *Psychology and Modern Life – Seventh Edition,* 35.

58 Gary R. Collins, *Christian Counseling: A Comprehensive Guide*, 298.

soul in the present. Protracted-traumatic stress is to perceive that the trauma is not a single event in the past, but rather an ongoing, recurring humiliation that must be defended against daily. Humiliations such as abuse, racism, sexism, classicism, poverty or any continuous form of dehumanizing oppression fall in this category.[59]

It is my considered opinion, based on sheer volume, that protracted traumatic stress for the abused and oppressed is potentially fortified due to ubiquitous and unlimited Internet access of causal stimuli, thus reinforcing the familiar abuse or oppression. In 2011 78% of the U.S. population, accessed the Internet weekly.[60] The average weekly access per individual in 2009 was 14 hours per week, not including email access.[61] Assuming an average awake time of 112 hours per week (8 hours per night of sleep per individual), approximately 12.5% of average time awake per individual is spent accessing the Internet.[62]

While increased Internet access leaves open the opportunity for negative external stimuli to the vulnerable, it also presents some unique opportunities for deviant behavior.[63] It confers new opportunities for deviance, such as the development of malware and virus ware, cyber-terrorism, computer hacking, online harassment, and certain self-destructive behaviors. With its ease of use and unbridled access to information, the Internet has facilitated and perpetuated existing crimes such as fraud, identity theft, and money laundering. As A.N. Joinson notes in *Deviance and the Internet: New Challenges for Social Science*, "People have

---

59 Lee. H. Butler, Jr., *Liberating our Dignity, Saving our Souls*, 182.

60 http://www.internetworldstats.com/stats.htm (Accessed December 15, 2011)

61 http://news.cnet.com/8301-1023_3-10421016-93.html (Accessed December 15, 2011)

62 http://www.sleepfoundation.org/article/how-sleep-works/how-much-sleep-do-we-really-need (Accessed December 15, 2011)

63 Marc Rogers, M., Natalie Smoak, N., & Jiu Liu, J. *Self-reported deviant computer behavior. Deviant Behavior: a big-5, moral choice, and manipulative exploitive behavior analysis*, 246.

always lied, cheated, and stolen, but the Internet enables some of them to do it more easily, quickly, and cheaply."[64]

The Internet also provides a fertile breeding ground for groups interested in extreme or negatively viewed behaviors.[65] Individuals can easily find others in cyberspace who share their deviant proclivities: pedophiles, people who actively seek sexually- transmitted diseases, self-injurers and hate groups, and these communities bestow reinforcing and validating benefits to users.[66] In short, the Internet is well-situated and well-suited to host a continuum of deviant behaviors.

In terms of corporate profit, the Internet is a huge driver of economic growth. In 2011 the Internet as a sector was about 3% of GDP, bigger than agriculture or energy, and represented over 20% of economic growth in the past 5 years, and still growing. For every job that the Internet destroys, 2.6 new net jobs are created.[67] Many of the jobs created are now globalized, thus impacting domestic job retention in the United State and contributing to an adjustment period of increased unemployment. As the church seeks to provide a holistic response to the aforementioned, it must do so with an understanding of how the Internet Generation (I-Generation) of souls in the boardrooms, and those affected by the boardrooms absorb and process information in the 21st century.

The I-Generation was born into a world where the Internet and mobile devices are a way of life. Devices like iPods, iPads, iPhones, iTouch, video games, multimedia, including instant access and real-time capabilities are literally at their fingertips.

---

64 Joinson, A. N. (2005*). Deviance and the internet: New challenges for social science*, 5–7.

65 Deshotels, T. H., & Forsyth, C. J. (2007). *Postmodern masculinities and the eunuch*, 201–218.

66 Adler, P. A., & Adler, P. (2008). *The cyber worlds of self-injurers: Deviant communities, relationships, and selves*, 33–56.

67 http://www.eg8forum.com/fr/documents/actualites/McKinsey_and_Company-internet_matters.pdf (Accessed December 15, 2011)

The multimedia and social media outlets to which this generation is accustomed open up an entirely new way of learning and absorbing information. The I-Generation is the first generation to be born into a world that uses computers for daily functions such as communicating through email, text, video chat, video talk, Skype, and other social media outlets like Facebook communication and tweeting with one or many persons, shopping, entertainment including playing video games, watching movies or favorite television shows, accessing the Internet, and blogging. The I-Generation learns and absorbs information differently than previous generations because of their access to technology and exposure to wireless mobile devices (WMB). Traditional learning and processing of information has changed.[68]

Research also shows that Internet users learn through multimedia presentations, which allows them to use their eyes, ears and the ability to touch to enhance their ability to receive information. Having technology that can be reviewed over and over, with the ability to rewind and focus on portions of presentations that may require more time to absorb, is a positive byproduct of increased use of technology. Internet users today with "multi-rich diets (using their auditory and visual senses), their love of video games (visual and tactile senses), and their multitasking use of computers and WMDs (more tactile and visual senses), possess the ability to learn and absorb through multimedia presentations that involve the three major senses."[69]

With consideration for the digital divide that widens the growing economic chasm between those who have and those who have not, the forgotten, the disenfranchised, and the yet un-awakened I-Generation, what and how will the digitally "connected city" as new creation serve as the instrument through which God will transform, redeem and restore individuals throughout an urbanizing world? How will the church evolve from protest to revolution, from prophetic voice to prophetic action toward uncompromised restoration? It is important not to confuse protest with revolution.

---

68 Larry D. Rosen, *Understanding the iGeneration and the Way They Learn*, 15.

69 Ibid., 16.

> Revolution is more than protest. Protest merely calls attention to injustice...It is in the act of defiance against what is conceived to be an established evil. It is the refusal to be silent in the presence of wrong to which others are accommodated. Social protest, while an initial step, flings a gauntlet into the teeth of a suspect authority and challenges the principles upon which that authority claims to rest.[70]

The church must now turn traditional implementation of theology upside down and inside out, while simultaneously overturning the tables of a digital urbanization that attacks the very freedom and liberation of persons. If the church is to affirm its freedom in God, it cannot do so by obeying laws, mediums, environments, and succumbing to circumstances that create and fortify oppression. By disobeying, the church not only affirms its role as a willing vessel for God but the humanity of both the oppressed and the oppressor.[71] A collaborative and theological roadmap for social change that must come from the church in response to each individual soul, with a goal of cultivating revolutionary wholeness is Romans 8:1-11. The Book of Romans is an unwavering, relentless, and revolutionary exhortation by the Apostle Paul. In this book the misguided earthly soul who was once the persecuting and murderous Saul has been converted and transformed to Paul, and impregnated with thanksgiving, so that he might embrace becoming a conduit, a vessel of continuous proclamation to the significance of the sacrificial death of our Lord and Savior Jesus Christ.

In this text, Paul has been changed and filled with the Holy Spirit so that at all times, with every moment that he breathed, with every temptation, with every thought, with every obstacle that he overcame, he would be spiritually worthy to stand before the almighty God, and enter His gates with thanksgiving and His courts with praise. And from then on Paul would praise God in

---

70 Cone, 136.

71 Ibid., 138.

whatever circumstance. So, too, must the 21st century church. When Paul was beaten, the very seed that God planted during that moment of transformation on that Damascus Road caused Paul's spirit to praise God. When Paul was imprisoned, he praised God. When Paul was persecuted, he trusted God. When Paul was placed on trial, he relied on God. When Paul was shipwrecked, he exalted God. When Paul was rejected by the world, he knew that greater was he that was in Him than he that was in the world. When Paul felt physical and emotional pain and anguish, he knew in his mind and in his heart that God's strength was made perfect in his greatest weakness. Every time that Paul was delivered it was not because Paul relied on others for that which was being denied, it was because Paul looked for strength from the God who walked with him, and talked with him, and slept with him, and who lived inside of him. No different than Paul, the 21st century church must do the same in the midst of global digital secularization, by finding a way to infuse the indwelling of the Holy Spirit in every individual, every organization, courtroom, jail house, and relationship through a collaborative network and ministry of presence.

In Romans, Paul's very life ahead of his unwavering proclamation shows the church that we block our final transformation and conversion and that of others when we choose to ignore the Spirit that God has provided to guide every believing soul. The church must convey to the world through thought, word and deed the importance of connection to the Spirit even and especially in the boardrooms. It is time for the church to be transient and unconventional, moving with an expectation of systemic change, no longer confined and shackled by the brick and mortar that surrounds the church every Sunday.

Romans Chapter 8 verse 1 states: "There is therefore now no condemnation to those who are in Christ Jesus, who do not walk according to the flesh, but according to the Spirit." In this verse Paul is proclaiming that God will not condemn us if we submit, if we do what Paul did, if we stop relying on the things that we can see and touch and feel in the earth. Paul is saying that we the church need to be transformed to become dependent on guidance from the Holy Spirit whom God put inside of each of us to fulfill our purpose here on earth. Paul wants each and every one of us to change our worldview. He wants us to focus our lives on prospering our relationship with Jesus Christ, rather than financial prosperity, or anything else.

But with all that we have learned and witnessed, so many in the church still ponder the question: How will we remain relevant, collaborative and focused when we are bombarded by a world that steps over the least of these; a world that chooses war over peace; a world that ignores unemployment, homelessness, domestic violence and unwarranted hate, a world that is filled with the darkness of moral apathy and spiritual bankruptcy? In Romans 8, God is not telling us to go to the world to receive light. God is telling us to take the light implanted inside of us to light up the entire world. Romans 8 verse 2 states: "For the law of the Spirit of life in Christ Jesus has made me free from the law of sin and death." In this text Paul is simply saying that we are justified by our faith through grace. No longer are we limited to eternal life based only on adherence to the laws of the Old Testament or the laws of the earth. He is saying that the path that frees each one of our spirits, away from our sinful bodies, our sinful natures, our fleshly desires, and eternal damnation, is belief in our minds and our hearts that Mary carried light into darkness to give birth in the manger, that God allowed death on the cross, burial in a borrowed tomb, and the resurrection of our Lord and Savior Jesus Christ for our redemption. Paul is trying to get us to understand that an immeasurable amount of our existence is our short time spent here on earth, which is the price that we must pay through righteousness, in order to experience the remainder of our eternal life in the Spirit with God. The church must now find a way to be revolutionary as a traditional and digital wholeness network of nurturing and healing, derived from the life of the religious community itself, from its worship and practice of prayer and meditation that shines a light that will always overcome earthly darkness.[72]

---

72 Margaret Kornfeld, *Cultivating Wholeness: A Guide to Care and Counseling in Faith Communities*, 69.

In Romans Chapter 8 verse 3 and 4, Paul goes on to say:

> [3] For what the law could not do in that it was weak through the flesh, God *did* by sending His own Son in the likeness of sinful flesh, on account of sin: He condemned sin in the flesh, [4] that the righteous requirement of the law might be fulfilled in us who do not walk according to the flesh but according to the Spirit.

In other words, if we are not constantly connected with the Holy Spirit, or God's conscience inside of us, offering up prayer and praise and thanksgiving to the almighty God, then it is impossible for our lives to be a witness of faith and belief. And because our salvation is justified by our faith through God's grace at the cross, our lives must remain a reflection of our faith and belief. When we choose not to show thanksgiving, sacrificing and seeking God, even for the little things in life, we compromise eternal life and salvation. And so the church must profess the giving of our bodies and ourselves as a holy and living sacrifice acceptable onto God, knowing that in all things God will make a way, somehow. At no time during the collaborative efforts of the church in healing, caregiving, and supportive activities throughout our communities can the church compromise its holiness.[73]

Central to this Romans pericope or section of the text in verse 5, Paul calls out both the believer and the non-believer; he says, "For those who live according to the flesh set their minds on the things of the flesh, but those *who live* according to the Spirit, the things of the Spirit." When we live according to the Spirit we defer instant gratification. We are suddenly able to walk away from those things and those habits that pull us away from God. When corporations accept this belief they begin to have a three-fold bottom line or commission starting with the well-being of their neighbor, their environment, and finally their economic stewardship to achieve the first two. The church need

---

73 Kornfeld, 70.

not shy away from its responsibility to be the clarion voice and conscience of corporations, organizations and society to establish a collaborative network of gifts and souls that reinforce love and peace in the world.

In verses 6 through 8 Paul goes on to say,

> For to be carnally-minded *is* death, but to be spiritually-minded *is* life and peace. [7] Because the carnal mind *is* enmity against God; for it is not subject to the law of God, nor indeed can be. [8] So then, those who are in the flesh cannot please God.

As the church, when we relinquish ourselves from ourselves, sacrificing and seeking God in every thing that we do, we then have unwavering assurance and peace. It is at that moment of authentic transformation that we go from hoping to knowing that no weapon formed against us shall prosper. It is in that harmonious place of bliss with God, of no worries, no fears, no pain, where we begin the unending and overflowing birth of unrealized thanksgiving. For we have the power to manifest God at all times, we have the power inside of ourselves to call on the Holy Spirit to please God, so that we might be more than conquerors through Him that sent us, knowing that in whatever circumstance we find ourselves, we can do all things through Christ who strengthens us.

As spirits housed in flesh, our spirits are yearning to give glory to God through our thoughts, our actions, and our willingness to serve TOGETHER, for verse 9 states: "But you are not in the flesh but in the Spirit, if indeed the Spirit of God dwells in you." Now if anyone does not have the Spirit of Christ, he is not His. If we do not rely on the Holy Spirit to guide our plans then we are not Children of God. Verses 10 and 11 of the text state: "And if Christ *is* in you, the body *is* dead because of sin, but the Spirit *is* life because of righteousness. But if the Spirit of Him who raised Jesus from the dead dwells in you, He who raised Christ from the dead will also give life to your mortal bodies through His Spirit who dwells in you." It is the absorption of verses 9 through 11 by the church that must progress from the church to transform and restore the I-Generation through a collaborative digital ministry platform that liberates all.

CHAPTER FOUR

Restore Together

The church in the 21st century must be the church of Jesus Christ with thorough consideration for global urbanization, digital secularization, the emerging I-Generation and the institutional sins of poverty and oppression. Institutional sin is sin that has infiltrated and accelerated erosion of every aspect of the eco-system of eternal life. Given such pervasive institutional sin, the understanding and approach of urban ministry taken by the church can no longer be limited solely to geography or local circumstance. Urban ministry must be a scalable and relentless approach by the church that addresses particular challenges and systemic causes with an expectation of mutual restoration. It must be a theology of social change that is at all times a revolutionary, collaborative, holistic and transformational Gospel response to the individual and the global community, wherever there is injustice or systematic oppression or disenfranchisement of those forgotten or negatively impacted by social, political, economic and religious structures. With exponential world hunger, environmental and agricultural resource depletion, the growing threat of nuclear war and institutional moral apathy, it is my contention that the church must begin to establish an Ark for the Remnant. This Ark solution is based on a treatise for the justification of psycho-spiritual war on poverty and oppression in the context of technology and energy in the 21st century, through the implementation of a ubiquitous yet peaceful digital platform that includes partners, advocates, strategic resources and education. The proposed platform should facilitate regional, local, and global collaboration and grass roots organization, in order to address the challenges of crisis response and reconciliation faced in the current reality of global urbanization.

Under the auspices of the "Fierce Urgency of Now," the treatise, a justification for psycho-spiritual war against poverty and oppression, is influenced by the underlying metaphor of Augustine's justification for war and the need to establish a non-violent platform that facilitates collaboration and reconciliation. This pre-emptive, pro-active and reactive digital community will incorporate a virtual framework that allows individual and corporate implementation of the four-step non-violent approach taken during the previously-mentioned Montgomery bus boycott, led by Rev. Dr. Martin Luther King, Jr. The adaptation of the phases of Dr. King's four-step method will include, not in any specific linear order:

1) Collection of the facts to determine whether injustices are alive;
2) Negotiation of modified circumstances that lead all parties to a place of sustainable healing and reconciliation;
3) Continuous self-purification and discipleship;
4) Direct non-violent action when applicable.[74]

The injustice or psycho-spiritual war that is alive within the Church today is its collective inability to effectively respond to crisis and oppression, inside and outside the church, due to a neo-colonialism that has caused tactical secularization and therefore spiritual separation of all parties. In this separation many of the oppressed are within the church, vulnerable and caught in a dysfunctional dialectical chasm between alienation theology (top down) and reconciliation theology (bottom up).[75] The bottom up theological perspective is based upon a behavioral orientation that reflects compassion, justice and a concern for society's most vulnerable (economically, educationally, ethnically, culturally,

---

74 Martin Luther King, Jr., *The Essential Writings and Speeches of Martin Luther King, Jr.*, 290.

75 Ronald E. Peters, *Urban Ministry: An Introduction*, 72.

physically, and spiritually).[76] The top down theological perspective refers to those whose social situation is comparatively secure, broadly affirmed and supported by the culture.[77] So there must be praxis through a committed effort of reconciliation, out of which the entire community (the oppressed and the oppressor) must come together through an integrated traditional and digital church to embrace the least of these in society.

Because the traditional church avoids confrontation with a digital secularization that infiltrates both the church and society, there is often a rationale for physical war because of the pre-emptive psycho-spiritual war the church refuses to justify. Rather than addressing the protracted traumatic stress disorder that is often resident in the subconscious of the oppressed, while also acknowledging the insecurities driving the oppressor, we respond only at the point of physical war. As King did in the Montgomery model, proactive and confrontational negotiation of modified circumstances that leads all parties to a place of sustainable healing and reconciliation must be at the forefront of any response from the church.

In review of Augustine's rationale for Christian participation in physical war based upon the duties of "neighbor love," he identifies and summarizes his explicit inclusion of just cause, legitimate authority and right intention in the requirements for a just war.[78] In response to Augustine's argument for Christian participation in physical war and with reference to the fall of Rome, I assert an exposition for reconciliation through justification of pre-emptive psycho-spiritual war, in an effort to avoid consideration for physical war. And in response to the justification of physical war, I propose unwavering sacrificial adherence to a platform of collaborative non-violence and peace.[79]

---

76 Ibid., 71.

77 Ibid., 75.

78 Sondra Wheeler. *Ethics – Formative Influences in the Christian Moral Tradition.* Class Notes 19 September, 2007.

79 David Ausburger, *The Freedom of Forgiveness,* 42.

As Augustine faced physical peril, in today's society the oppressed face an ingrained dehumanizing poverty resulting from a relentless and digitally charged neo-colonialism. Augustine lived through the decline and fall of the Roman Empire. The city of Rome was sacked and burned and citizens were rounded up and slaughtered. In the years between two and three hundred and the late fourth century, the position of the church moved dramatically from being ignored, radically persecuted and intentionally marginalized to becoming the official religion, and ultimately a central part of the civil service function within the society. After the sacking of Rome, the Church was the only non-local institution left standing. The church tended to the flood of refugees when Roman outposts were burned. The church cared for the orphans. The Church took on welfare functions as it sought to care for people, and it dealt with social order that made human life possible. After the church had inherited the management of civil power, suddenly the management of violence would also become the church's affair.[80] This was a change because in an earlier era, Christians benefited by the free order infused by Rome's military but they refused to bear arms; they were parasitic on social order.

When Augustine inherits this unprecedented role in society he has to figure out what Christian responsibility is in terms of "the neighbor" in the face of this disaster. So, too, must today's church as it relates to "the neighbor" in the context of the dehumanizing poverty and oppression that is growing globally. What Augustine does is to develop the first theological defense of Christian participation in violence. For Augustine it is not only permitted but it is a Christian duty and obligation to protect the neighbor. Augustine views the obligation as the right love of God or the right love of Jesus through the love of neighbor rather than self-defense. So Augustine develops this defense of the use of lethal force by a Christian. Augustine believed that if a Christian's assailant is about to perish in his or her sins and we who are Christians can afford to die, self-defense is not permitted. We do

---

80 Sondra Wheeler. Ethics – *Formative Influences in the Christian Moral Tradition*. Class Notes 19 September, 2007.

not go to war for ourselves but only for the sake of other citizens who are not Christian and not ready to go to heaven. He believed that we go to war or use force for the sake of those who do not love and know the truth and therefore are subject to judgment. "He believed that we must resort to force in order to maintain the conditions of human social life, in order that the Gospel can continue to do its work, and for all of those who will be brought under the dominion of the truth."[81]

Augustine's underlying motivation was neighbor love with a strategy of maintaining order. "Augustine will take tyranny over chaos."[82] He asserted that human beings require order to sustain life, and that social order is a necessity since human life is inherently and permanently social. He believed that social order cannot be compromised, and that the maintenance of some kind of social order is necessary for existence. He asserted that Christians are inclined to love their neighbors and that love of a neighbor who needs order for love, mandates Christian preservation in the establishment of order. It is not favor to let a wrongdoer or a murderer go free. It is far better to constrain and limit the evildoer; perhaps it can birth good. And so Augustine justifies war under the following conditions: explicit inclusion of just cause, legitimate authority and right intention.[83]

A just cause for Augustine is an aggressive attacker that jeopardizes the survival of the community. He also entertains the idea that you might resort to war to punish a wrong doer. He believed that war in order to be justified must be in response to evil or in response to aggression. According to Augustine, people go to war to obtain peace. I assert that the 21st century church must initiate a preemptive war of peace against the aggression of those evil factors that facilitate a dehumanizing poverty and oppression that may result in all out physical war. Augustine believed that legitimate authority is whoever has responsibility

81 Ibid.

82 Wheeler.

83 Ibid.

for the welfare of the whole.[84] I assert that the church has the moral responsibility and accountability for the welfare of the whole. He also believed that the only legitimate aim for war is the restoration of peace, and war must be directed based on legitimate authority.

According to Augustine, along with just cause and last resort, wars must have right intention. Christians cannot inflict harm for self. In order to go to war, there must be a desire for restoration of peace. His motivation for participation in war is the love of neighbor. Although you may be willing to attack the aggressor, you are not permitted to hate the aggressor. Hatred is a sin, you must intervene to stop the evil, particularly on behalf of those who are not ready to meet God, but there is no room for hate. You may not aim to destroy as an end, although destruction may be a necessary means to end evil.

As contemporary Christians we often take for granted that we have a moral as well as a legal right to self-defense, not an obligation to be obedient as ambassadors of reconciliation.[85] Our motivation for war is based first on a presumed right of self-preservation and not on the love of neighbor. Historically, our response to aggression or perceived threat has been war. The current U.S. Military Doctrine for the Justification for War (just cause, last resort, legitimate authority, right intention, balance of justice, reasonable hope for success, proportionality) is without motivation for the love of the non-believing neighbor. Augustine's justification for the use of lethal force based on neighbor love has been shifted to the contemporary secular justification for the use of lethal force (motivated by self-preservation) in response to aggression.

From the time of Augustine until now, history has proven that physical war and oppression will ultimately beget more physical war and more oppression. History also shows that if the approach is not peaceful and not consistent with the desired ends, then the solution will become a cancer that compounds the problem,

---

84 Ibid.

85 Wheeler.

accelerating spiritual and physical annihilation. "Physical fighting for the sake of peace is like fornicating for the sake of virginity."[86] And so I feel with consideration for history and Augustine's justification for war that we are called to pro-actively neutralize the possibility of poverty- and oppression-driven wars as prophetic agents of Christian transformation, and to address crisis through a collaborative digital platform of love and peace.

Through collaborative traditional and digital ministry between the oppressed and the oppressor toward the least of these in society, continuous self-purification and discipleship must fortify our submission that God is the initiator of reconciliation and we are the beneficiaries. Our calling is to give testimony by imitating God and making reconciliation real in the world. A Christian is an ambassador of reconciliation. The ministry of a Christian is reconciliation. As Christians we should approach all enemies from a position of peace, humility, and restoration. 2 Corinthians 5:17-20 says,

> Therefore, if anyone is in Christ, he is a new creation; old things have passed away; behold all things have become new. [18] Now all things are of God, who has reconciled us to Himself through Jesus Christ, and has given us the ministry of reconciliation, [19] that is, that God was in Christ reconciling the world to Himself, not imputing their trespasses to them, and has committed to us the word of reconciliation. [20] Now then, we are ambassadors for Christ, as though God were pleading through us: we implore you on Christ's behalf, be reconciled to God.

Reconciliation is not conditional, it is not just verbal forgiveness, it is physical communication, it is sacrifice and suffering, it is asserting peace and it is transparent interaction toward individual and corporate resolution with God. Reconciliation with God is represented by love of our neighbors including our

---

86 Wheeler.

enemies based on our actions.[87] Christ suffered but he forgave on the cross so that we might be reconciled, for in 1 Peter 2:21-24 it is written,

> For to this you were called, because Christ also suffered for us, leaving us an example, that you should follow His steps: [22] " Who committed no sin, Nor was deceit found in His mouth"; [23] who, when He was reviled, did not revile in return; when He suffered, He did not threaten, but committed Himself to Him who judges righteously; [24] who Himself bore our sins in His own body on the tree, that we, having died to sins, might live for righteousness by whose stripes you were healed.

As Christians we must be transformed by the renewing of our minds to respond peacefully in thought and in action, by suffering and persevering until authentic forgiveness and reconciliation is achieved. Matthew 5:38-39 tells us, "You have heard that it was said, 'An eye for an eye and a tooth for a tooth.' But I tell you not to resist an evil person. But whoever slaps you on your right cheek, turn the other to him also." Further, Matthew 5:43-45 go on to say,

> You have heard that it was said, 'You shall love your neighbor and hate your enemy.' [44] But I say to you, love your enemies, bless those who curse you, do good to those who hate you, and pray for those who spitefully use you and persecute you, [45] that you may be sons of your Father in heaven; for He makes His sun rise on the evil and on the good, and sends rain on the just and on the unjust.

---

87 Don Baker, *Beyond Forgiveness: The Healing Touch of Church Discipline* (Chicago: University of Chicago Press, 1999), 34.

Matthew 6:14-15 states, "For if you forgive men their trespasses, your heavenly Father will also forgive you. [15] But if you do not forgive men their trespasses, neither will your Father forgive your trespasses." We must reconcile in a spirit of peace and of love regardless of the circumstance. 1 John 4:20 says, "If someone says, 'I love God,' and hates his brother, he is a liar; for he who does not love his brother whom he has seen, how can he love God whom he has not seen?"

I can find no comprehensive biblical basis in the New Testament that supports Augustine's use of lethal force in response to evil aggression. I feel that social order is critical to human survival but obedience to God takes precedence. In my opinion, aggressive non-violent resistance and action based on the love of neighbor is the obligation of the Christian. The Christian should take this non-violent action out of desired reconciliation with God for the evildoer, the believer or the non-believer, the oppressed or the oppressor. As Christians we are obligated to respond to evil aggression with assertive non-violence toward reconciliation, even when facing physical annihilation. I believe that our approach must be consistent with our desired ends and that lasting peace can only be obtained through peaceful methods. In our response to evil aggression there must be right intention and that right intention must be reconciliation. The aim for non- violent response is the restoration, peace and welfare of the whole.

With consideration for the aforementioned, we must always let our conscience be our guide. As stated by Reinhold Niebuhr in his theologically world-changing book, *Moral Man and Immoral Society*, "The limitations of the human mind and imagination, the inability of human beings to transcend their own interests sufficiently to envisage the interests of their fellow-men as clearly as they do their own makes force an inevitable part of the process of social cohesion. But the same force which guarantees peace may make for injustice."[88] He goes on to say, "The most perfect justice cannot be established if the moral imagination of the indi-

---

88 Reinhold Niebuhr, *Moral Man and Immoral Society: A study in Ethics and Politics* 6.

vidual does not seek to comprehend the needs and interests of his fellows. Any justice which is only justice soon degenerates into something less than justice."[89] Our first priority must be the soul salvation of our brothers and sisters through non-violent action.

During the Civil rights movement quite often the platform for direct non-violence for the church was marching in demonstrations and boycotting. In the early 21st century the medium for direct non-violent action, the medium that quite often reflects the conscience of God's people, giving attention to the prophetic voice, is the Internet.

The thrust of this book is the development and implementation of the "Restore Together Community." It is time for the church to restore God's people together through a digital ministry/platform community (internet, desktop, laptop, smart-phone, etc.) that is dynamic, collaborative, multilingual and accessible to individuals with disabilities, while enhancing giving organization's gifts/resources, ability to provide holistic counseling, discipleship, sharing of best practices, and ability to organize community action. The "Restore Together Community" must allow giving and receiving of donations (for organizations only), gift cards, products (food, shelter, clothing), services (legal, accounting, marketing, construction, etc.), and commodity (electricity, power, gas, water, etc.) for organizations and individuals in need, globally. The financial profits from this community will be used to erase the digital/energy divide for the deeply impoverished by allowing people in collaborative communion to liberate each other through loving sacrifice and daily praxis.

---

89 Niebuhr, 257.

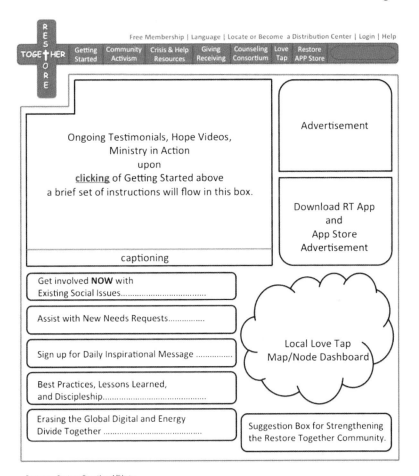

Getting Started | Community Activism | Crisis & Help Resources | Giving Receiving | Counseling Consortium | Love Tap | Restore APP Store

Ongoing Testimonials, Hope Videos,
Ministry in Action
upon
clicking of Getting Started above
a brief set of instructions will flow in this box.

captioning

Advertisement

Download RT App
and
App Store
Advertisement

Get involved **NOW** with
Existing Social Issues...................................

Assist with New Needs Requests...............

Sign up for Daily Inspirational Message ....

Best Practices, Lessons Learned,
and Discipleship...

Erasing the Global Digital and Energy
Divide Together ....

Local Love Tap
Map/Node Dashboard

Suggestion Box for Strengthening
the Restore Together Community.

Become a Restore Together Affiliate....
Become a Restore Together Certified Distribution Center
Advertise your organization

For example, a pastor is deeply frustrated by lack of success in reaching younger generations in the congregation and seeks best practices that are relevant to their specific circumstances. The pastor uses the best practices worship and discipleship postings from the Restore Together Community that are relevant. The Pastor also engages the younger generation through the hundreds of ministry apps available for download from the Restore Together App Store.

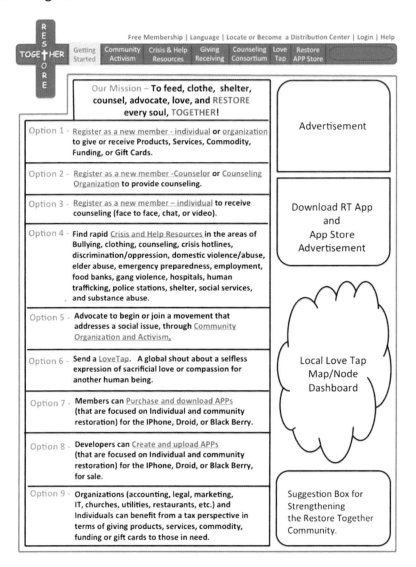

In the Restore Together Community when the inexperienced pastor is faced with responding to a newly experienced human trafficking crisis in his or her congregation in the middle of the night, the pastor reaches out to the Restore Together (RT) Community through his or her smartphone to receive best practices, real-time feedback from pastors in Korea, Mexico and the Bronx who have had similar experiences. The RT Community automatically translates the correspondence. The pastor is also able to identify relevant crisis programs through the community database and is able to locate clinical counseling resources and 24/7 safe-houses to address the immediate crisis, all while establishing a holistic ministry approach to address the middle of the night challenge long-term. Both the recipient and the pastor will receive ongoing daily scriptural correspondence of hope and encouragement from RT.

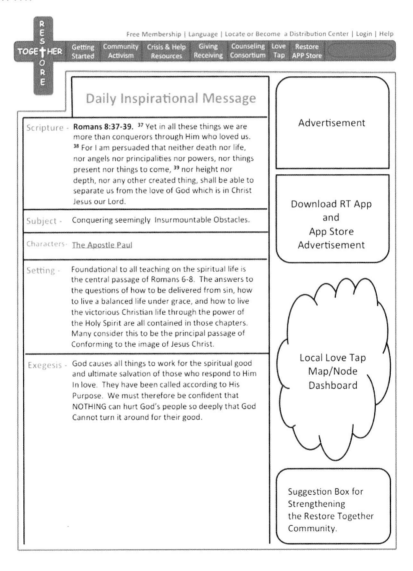

A Korean- or Spanish-speaking church is looking to work in seamless collaboration with other English speaking churches and organizations in the Restore Together Community to make a difference in the lives of their communities and their congregants.

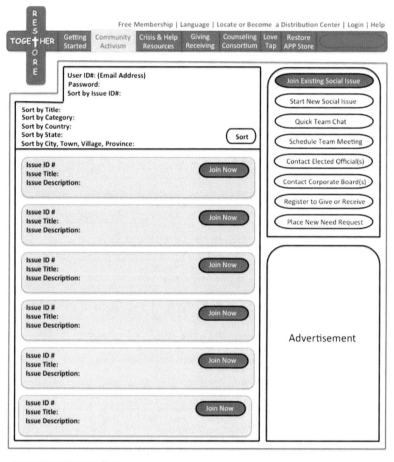

Become a Restore Together Affiliate....
Become a Restore Together Certified Distribution Center
Advertise your organization

A church, homeless shelter, organization or individual wants to call out injustice in the prison-industrial complex such as capital punishment, while providing holistic resources (employment, counseling, etc.) to reduce recidivism. Through community activism, corporate entities that invest in the prison-industrial complex are publicly approached to provide training and employment that will decrease recidivism. The Restore Together Community is also used to address systemic change by collectively approaching local and congressional lawmakers who define disproportionate prison sentencing, and capital punishment guidelines. Through collaborative correspondence within the RT community, an organic plan for systemic and particular change is established.

A previously troubled school is being re-built in a deeply impoverished community, and is in need of crisis resources for troubled families, volunteers, corporate expertise, accounting, architectural and construction resources. The school can receive assistance through community activism in the RT Community, and donated accounting, legal, construction and marketing services from partner organizations of the RT Community. The RT Community will also allow collaboration with local churches for after-school and family programs, all with an expectation that the schools' employees and graduates will be encouraged to, at some point, make positive volunteer contributions in the local community.

A homeless shelter is in need of additional resources as Federal and State programs that previously assisted are no longer available. The shelter, through the Restore Together Community, is able to receive surplus clothing from Nordstrom's, Bloomingdales; surplus Food from Wal-Mart; donated counseling services from the Christian Counseling Consortium that is a part of the RT Community; and formalization of a weekly worship and discipleship program through partnership with local churches. All of the secular contributing individuals and organizations immediately receive tax form receipts upon mutual acknowledgment of service, commodity or product distribution on-line, reflecting their contributions. Each serving or giving organization is encouraged not only to serve but to ensure their policies, practices and behavior are in line ethically with restoration of all souls within their organization and those souls touched by the missions of their organizations.

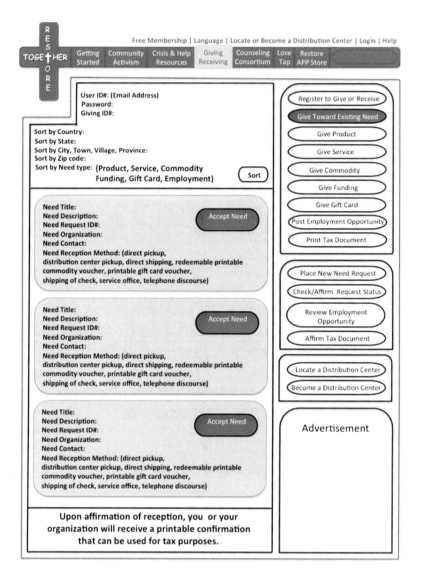

A large number of churches from different denominations and beliefs have never come together to make a consistent difference in the gang-influenced communities where they co-exist and serve. Through collaboration in the RT Community, the ecumenical church community begins to plan and act upon intense counseling and loving programs with a focus of positive infiltration and transformation of the gang presence throughout the community, starting not only with the gang members but their schools and, most importantly, their families.

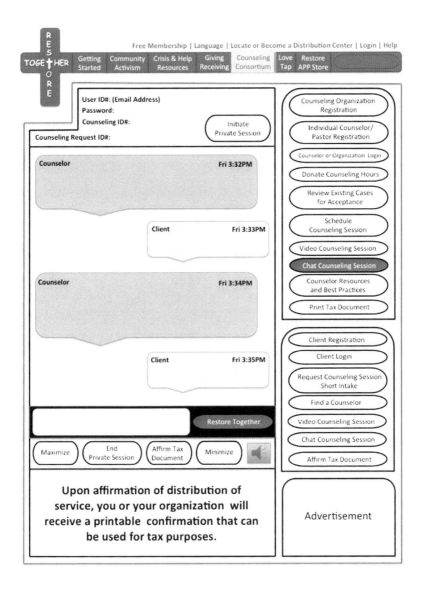

A deeply impoverished blind or deaf person in West Virginia has heard or seen negative news all day through television, newspapers and radio, and they are in need of hearing or seeing something positive in the world. By clicking on the love tap content that is accessible to the blind, low-vision and hearing-impaired in the Restore Together Community, they can listen or read texts (LoveTap™) about positive expressions of sacrificial love for other human beings globally.

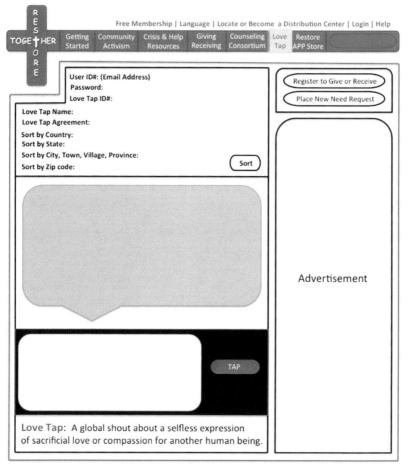

A person is in need of hope and seeking emergency and food resources after climbing out of the rubble from an earthquake. They bring up a Global Information System (GIS) Crisis Application on their smartphone that was downloaded from the hundreds of Apps in the Crisis section of the Restore Together Apps Store. The Application directs them to available churches, hospitals, police stations, first-aid locations and shelters based on global locations that can be navigated independent of street obstruction from flooding and other structural impediments. This person is sent scriptural hope and encouraging correspondence throughout the ordeal.

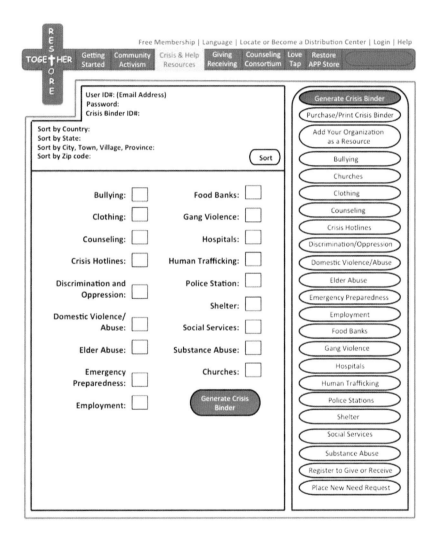

The Restore Together Community is a ubiquitous digital ministry platform for waging peaceful war on oppression, poverty, and institutional sin, globally. The platform supports a theology of social change by allowing users to collect the facts to determine whether injustices are alive through investigation, organization and activism. The Restore Together Community provides collaborative resources and methods for physical and virtual action by all parties through giving and receiving, crisis resources, counseling, and a dynamic portal of mobile applications that support the premise of allowing negotiation of modified circumstances that lead all parties to a place of sustainable healing and reconciliation. And finally it is a peaceful non-violent community that provides continuous discipleship and best practices toward continuous self-purification.

As Christ raised Lazarus, we must become inspired to rise out of the rubble and start a journey toward resurrection from spiritual separation, toward collaborative restoration by coming together in community, the haves the have-nots, the oppressed and the oppressor, to assist the least of these throughout the new Internet global city. Through the catalyst of crisis and the praxis of problem-posing education I pray that we may finally begin to acknowledge the broader challenges of division that we face, and that we begin to awaken from the normative gaze.

As we begin to collaborate and rise out of the spiritual tomb that incarcerates our collective purpose and prevents us from a true restoration, and a sure resurrection of hope and promise, I pray that God will use our collective response to remove our shared stones: the stone of hate, the stone of insecurity, the stone of doubt, the stone of fear, the stones of isolation and separation, the stone of condemnation, the stone of laziness, the stone of biblical illiteracy, the stone of unfaithfulness, the stone of bitterness, the stone of complacency, the stone of moral apathy, the stone of cynicism, the stone of non-preparation, the stone of deceit, the stone of hypocrisy, the stone of oppression, the stone of abuse, the stone of greed, the stone of divisiveness, and the stone of inconsistency.

And as the many stones are being removed so that our brothers and sisters who had been left for dead under the rubble might be made whole, a transformational love will respond within the subconscious of every soul touched in and through this growing community of submission. Going forward it is my prayer that we may become "Boundary Leaders" and learn something of the skills for leadership that Gary Gunderson talks about in his book by that name. My hope with this proposed program of Restore Together Community (http://restoretogether.com) is to fortify our unity through relationship webs that sustain, encourage, and transform, so that we might find the lasting resilience, reconciliation and even the full manifestation of God's power through our sacrificial love for one another.[90]

---

90 Gary Gunderson, *Boundary Leaders: Leadership Skills for People of Faith,* 155.

CHAPTER FIVE

Repairing the Breach

Case Study 1: Organizing Community for Reconciliation
Case Study 2: i-Generation Transformation
Case Study 3: Building the Restore Together Community

Isaiah 58:12 states, [12]Those from among you shall build the old waste places; you shall raise up the foundations of many generations; and you shall be called the repairer of the breach, the restorer of streets to dwell in." According to this scripture, the repairers of the breach are the watchmen who cry out and spare not.[91] They lift up their voices and show God's people their transgression and sin against God's moral law of love.[92] The repairers of the breach are laborers guided by the hands of God, to loosen the bonds of wickedness, undo the heavy burdens, and break every yoke that binds mankind in sin.[93] They teach and preach God's holy law of the Spirit of life and liberty.[94] They further give spiritual and physical bread to the hungry, shelter to the homeless, and they clothe the naked with the robe of the righteousness, which is of God by faith.[95] The light of God's righteousness is upon them, and when they call on the Lord His unfailing answer is "Here I am."[96]

---

91 Isaiah 58:12

92 Isaiah 58:1

93 Isaiah 58:6

94 Isaiah 58:7

95 Isaiah 58:8

96 Isaiah 58:9

The Lord guides them continually, and waters them so abundantly that they are like a spring of water themselves.[97]

The word breach in the text "the repairer of the breach" means according to the Hebrew "a break," or "a gap." So what is relevant for the church in the midst of global urbanization today? When we look at verse 1 of Isaiah 58 we see that God is commanding that a loud cry be sounded among His people showing them their transgression and sins. These scriptures are not obsolete, but rather are a command to God's faithful watchmen today to sound a loud cry and lift up their voices like a trumpet calling out all their transgressions and sins. This can only be done through revelation and an active praxis of God's perfect law of love.

The following three case studies were used to examine the use of the Internet as a tool to achieve God's perfect law of love in action.

Case Study 1: Organizing Community for Reconciliation.

At the beginning of the Urban Ministry Doctoral program at Wesley Theological Seminary during the first track taught by Dr. Fred Smith, it became clear to my spirit that the very community and program from which we would learn and serve was itself in need of transparent reconciliation. As a result, I spoke out at the end of the first class and recommended to both Dr. Smith and my fellow doctoral candidates that we would not and could not leave the program as we entered, that we must become authentic agents of restorative and reconciling change. As a result of obedience to the spirit, I was asked by Dr. Smith and my classmates to lead an initiative that would shed light and bring about healing and reconciliation. I began to organize twelve of my classmates by setting up a Yahoo-groups account for chat, email, document integration and document sharing during our semesters in class, and in between semesters for continuous communication, planning and collaboration. I also went online to establish a free (800) conference call number that facilitated more than thirty conference

---

97 Isaiah 58:11

calls with classmates around the country that I led in order to discuss and coordinate the case study. Finally, I used email to facilitate scheduling of face-to-face meetings and presentations to those parties in the partnership who would be affected by the case study.

The case study sought to assist one particular partnership, located at the center of the city, to become a spiritual balm of healing, a mecca for information, and a model for transformative community change. Inspired by the vision of the Beloved Community, Wesley Theological Seminary, Asbury United Methodist Church, Mount Vernon Place United Methodist Church [MVP-UMC], Mount Vernon Place, and the Downtown Cluster of Churches formed a partnership: The Urban Ministry and Community Transformation Initiative [UMCT or Partnership] within the nation's capital. The Partnership's focus was urban ministry and effecting a change in the current landscape and conditions. Within this urban complex that consists of power, privilege, prosperity, poverty and the poor, there is promising opportunity to reform, restore, redeem, and reconcile people and community in an effort to renew, transform, and cultivate wholeness.[98]

Since the establishment of the partnership, it was apparent that, as with many new ventures, there was a need to re-evaluate the existing partnership to ensure its mission, vision, goals and objectives were on track. The intent of the case study was to conduct a thoughtful analysis, offer realistic recommendations, actions, steps and strategies that could ultimately create a shared vision among partners. The shared vision and activities focused on systemic change.

In January 2010, as a part of Wesley's Call to the City, this Urban Ministry initiative had a two-fold mission intended to:

- Embed seminary students and the school in community in an effort to create a spiritual presence in the city and develop partnerships with local stakeholders, and;

---

98 Urban Ministry D.Min. Student Collaboration – Praxis Elective Final Submission – May 2011

- Establish an Urban Ministry doctoral track that would serve as a hands-on learning laboratory where ministerial practitioners would be able to both study and effect a positive change in the community.

Specifically, Wesley's Urban Ministry initiative was centered on contextual education, predicated on the belief that ministry is understood and carried out in context. As such, Wesley's urban ministry doctoral students "learn to engage the poor and the powerful, to meet the needs of diverse cultures, and to answer their call to dynamic, applied ministry in the complex social systems of the inner-city."[99] As part of the doctoral program's Urban Ministry track, students were divided into groups, assigned to one of the partnership organizations and charged to conduct a social critical analysis and offer thoughtful analysis and recommendations. What once was a single semester assignment became a two-year engagement and case study to assist the partnership in establishing a realistic shared vision, mission and plan that the full complement of participants would collaboratively work to advance.[100]

What follows is a snapshot of this process, which includes a collaborative analysis based on feedback from each partnering organization, along with integrated recommendations and strategies for the partners. It was our hope that this approach would enable partners to depart from the appearance of a closed, 'stove-piped' organizational mentality, trapped by tradition, hierarchy, paternalism and exclusive structures to a process that is visibly open, welcoming, transformative, inclusive, and collaborative.[101]

---

99 Call to the City, Wesley Theological Seminary Website, June 15, 2011

100 Urban Ministry D.Min. Student Collaboration – Praxis Elective Final Submission – May 2011

101 Urban Ministry D.Min. Student Collaboration – Praxis Elective Final Submission – May 2011

The collaborative analysis of all organizations within the partnership showed:

- There were no visible signs of an existing partnership
- Parties desired to and were willing to work together
- Everyone needed to come to the table and agree on a shared vision, mission, goals and objectives and develop a plan of action
- The partnership lacked the apparent need for trust and relationship that is the spirit of the Beloved Community
- Partnerships are to serve the public good through transparency, fidelity, dialogue, relationship building and reconciliation; all are critical elements among partners and central to this partnership in general.
- There was ambiguity in the roles and expectations of Mount Vernon Square Urban Ministry Project Partners.
- There was a need to establish parity and equity within the ministry partnership structure.
- Concern for Financial investment and return on investment of partners
- Valuing the contributions and historical legacies of all partner organizations was lacking.
- In terms of Wesley Theological Seminary, the urban ministry prong of their three-prong approach to the Mt Vernon project appeared to be the least thought out, but the most marketed.
- There was a need for clarity of communication when it came to vision and process.
- One prominent emblem of contention for Asbury United Methodist Church is visible and is found in the deeply etched words in six-inch letters on the marble entrances of Mount Vernon Place UMC which reads, "Methodist Episcopal Church, South." The Bishop of the Area at the time suggested that the words should stay so that the church's history, albeit painful, would not be swept under the rug. However, both that decision and the church's decision were possibly based

on the cost-prohibitive nature [$80,000] involved in removing these words. In particular the word "South," which summons painful memories of exclusivity when the Methodist Church split over the issue of slavery, had the potential to widen the cleavage between the two churches.

Throughout the case study there were several biblical motifs that were apparent in the dynamic evolution of the partnership:

1) The Nehemiah Motif: using the power and influence of the King's House to rise up and rebuild;
2) Repairers of the Breach (Isaiah 58: 6-12); and the most dominant
3) The Passion, and Crucifixion of Jesus Christ

The following questions were posed to the partners based on the case study: What will our work and souls in this collaborative tell Jesus *'on that great getting up morning?'* At the center of the city when the homeless come, and the sick cry out, and the poor reach out, and the corrupt infiltrate, and hate threatens — Beloved Shalom Community, we must ask ourselves the question individually and collectively: are we the Christian servants of social change or should they look for another? When the remnant comes seeking the collective sacrifice that God expected from us before time existed, will our collective cross be vacant? Where is the prophetic voice and action of the partnership? Are we the Christian healing balm or should they look for another?

At the end of the case study the following recommendations and strategies for transformative action and change were made to the partnership:

- Define the partnership and communicate its vision, mission and goals.
- Acknowledge partners' expectations
- Review the process of establishing the partnership, who are the key players and who is missing

- Conduct an Open House and provide information to community businesses and organizations about the community services provided at Mount Vernon Square.
- Engage in a community healing dialogue addressing, cultural, racial, ethnic and social conflict that strains relationships-*"an environment in which true compassion, reconciliation, restitution, and right relationship" occur*. An outside professional facilitator should be secured.
- Interface with the Washington DC Area Neighborhood Commissions and other local highly connected persons in the community, neighborhood "Mavens" and community visioning teams.
- Establish a joint action team consisting of members and leaders of both congregations be developed to provide ministry to the surrounding community. Creating a Web of Transformation" and seek the input of the community, business, faith, etc.
- That MVP UMC should gift space and or resources to Asbury UMC.
- To have a series called Season of Exchange and Collaboration with Wesley, MVP UMC and Asbury UMC [i.e., pulpit exchanges, learning series, shared ministries, etc.]
- Adapt Ronald Peter's benevolent model and the belonging model of doing Urban Ministry: create a partnership that reflects a belonging paradigm and one that empowers voice and influence from the bottom-up.
- Provide opportunities for Christian and continuing education which is vital to church growth and development. These extend beyond Bible study and Sunday School that transform people into effective leaders and contributors of the community and society.
- Identify tools to aid in effective life application of the Word of God. Contemporary life issues such as homelessness, substance abuse and addiction, financial management, spousal abuse, and other personal and social challenges must be incorporated in the Christian and continuing education module.

- Make available the governing documents used to formulate the strategic vision and how that relates to the implementation of the plan.
- Understand the importance of shared concern and shared power. Wesley has the ability to empower these partners and it should do so to build the Beloved Community.
- Establish a Practice in Ministry and Mission (PMM) site with the Downtown Cluster of Congregations to allow Urban Ministry fellows and other students the opportunity to learn community organizing at the practical level.
- Include cultural competency and cultural awareness training and discussions in the curriculum for Urban Ministry students, including Master of Divinity and Doctor of Ministry programs. This training should encompass the dynamics of racism, homophobia, xenophobia, classism, and sexism, and privilege.
- Expand the sample of the participatory action research to include more congregations of color and various sizes/denominations and non-denominations by tapping into additional networks.
- Include in the research activities of the Urban Fellows Program, studies of the residential communities and their needs. Such research would not be limited to computer generated data gathering, but would primarily include fact-to-face inquiries, group forums, and pavement-based environmental analysis and relationship building.
- Establish an Urban Ministry Center at Mount Vernon Square
- Embrace Urban Ministry Doctoral students as Ministry Practitioners and ethnographers engaged in hands-on, action-oriented service, research and community-faith organizing. Invite, include and embrace.

In conclusion, during the two years of the case study, I found a willingness of the majority of the parties involved to work together. The case study was made possible through the use of the Internet, which accelerated communication, a cross-country collaboration of resources, research, documentation integration, and real-time encouragement. The collective prophetic voice was heard.

Case Study 2: i-Generation Transformation.

On November 15, 2011 my daughter Naya (11 years old at the time) approached my wife (Rev. Demetra Hutchinson) and me in a matter-of-fact tone to let us know that she had accomplished all goals associated with her academics, her dancing in the Washington Ballet, her chores around the house, her bible study, and her relationships with both family and friends. And based on such accomplishment, she had taken the time to review multiple catalogs and information online, from which she provided us a highlighted and extensive printed list of the many items that she EXPECTED to receive under the tree for Christmas! After taking a deep breath, I calmly looked at my wife, and through the power of the Holy Spirit I said, "Naya, before we can discuss what you will receive for Christmas you need to experience the power of giving, and so you have just volunteered to be a case study in my doctoral project. Tomorrow I need you to submit a letter to your Principal requesting that he allow you to lead a coat drive for the entire school, which you will lead and organize at your school for distribution to the homeless when we go out in a couple of weeks." The next morning, as she did the night before when campaigning for her desired Christmas items, she went online using the Internet to submit the following email to the Principal, Larry of Friends Community School in College Park, Maryland:

> Dear Larry,
> Every Christmas my family and I go to feed the homeless outside in the parks of the District of Columbia. But every time we go there are children that are my age, cold and hungry. It is sad because we never have enough coats for all of them.
> I was wondering if somehow we could ask the whole middle school to collect coats over a period of time (November 10th – December 9th). I believe that we can collect 50 to 75 coats in this short amount of time.

One way of letting the middle school students know that I will be collecting any spare coats that they have is through middle school meeting. And I am requesting that a notice be included in the school's weekly bulletin. Every time someone brings in a jacket they can put it in a bin or box I will have in my advisory (Anne's advisory). I believe that the middle school students will be very motivated to do this and help people who are less fortunate than them.
Sincerely,
Naya A. Hutchinson

Two days after she submitted the letter to Principal Larry, he enthusiastically approved. The next morning she sent a text to five of her classmates to request their assistance in volunteering to create signs to post around the school, and to decorate boxes for the coat drive. The principal also provided Naya the opportunity to stand up at the weekly meeting for worship in front of the entire school in order to mention the coat drive, and the principal also submitted Naya's original letter that he had received as a part of the weekly online electronic bulletin that is emailed to all faculty, employees, parents and students.

November 18, 2011 FCS eBulletin
FCS Student-Run Coat Drive

Hi, my name is Naya Hutchinson and I am in 7th grade here at FCS. Every year my family donates coats and feeds the homeless during the holidays. Even after all of our efforts, each year there are children who are the same ages of students at FCS and some adults who are not able to receive coats since we run out of them. This year it is my goal to collect more coats and warm more people during this cold season. I am seeking the help of my schoolmates and FCS community to help me meet this goal.

Here's what you can do:
- Bring in spare coats that you do not use
- There will be a bin in the lobby where you can drop the coats off
- Coats will be collected November 20th - December 9th

Thank you in advance for your support,
Naya Hutchinson

The coats began to pile in, and by December 9th there were over 100 coats ranging in sizes from toddler to large adults. The transformation from requestor to giver was starting. Naya and her younger brother, Louis IV, then pushed her mother and me to move forward with a Holiday Party where the attendees would

have a dessert contest and would make up food bags for the homeless, and Naya, Louis IV and friends would bake cookies, and print encouraging scripture verses to go inside the bags for the homeless. And so Naya and her mother worked on an Evite to send out to many of the Friends Community School families, neighborhood families and others friends and family for a party on December 30, 2011. Over 100 invitees accepted, including 40 children. On that night the children filled sandwich bags for the homeless with fruit, 558 home-baked cookies, chips, candy, and water. Adults cut out scripture quotes with additional social services resource information to place in the bags. The adults also organized coats by category: Men, Women, Teens, Youth and Toddlers that Naya and her grandmother had previously washed and sewn, where needed.

The following morning, Saturday, December 31, 2011 starting at breakfast, six of the families, including the children, returned to car-

avan to the park at 13th and I Streets, NW in DC, to assist our family in distribution. When we arrived in the park we held hands and I prayed in the middle of a giant spiral circle with over 250 homeless persons, "that the food delivered represent the broken body of our Lord and Savior Jesus Christ, and that the water they drink represent Jesus' spilled blood for the remission of their sins..." Within 35 minutes we distributed 186 lunch bags of food, water, toiletry items, garbage bags, over 100 coats, hats, socks, scarfs and gloves that we had purchased and collected. The park that had been filled with despair had, for at least a short time, been converted to a sanctuary of hope and love by the efforts of the I-Generation. Upon Naya's arrival back to school after the Christmas break she submitted a thank you email to Principal Larry, which he then synopsized and conveyed to the FCS Community. He also provided a hand-written thank you letter directly to Naya. My eleven-year-old daughter benefited tremendously by responding to the challenge to give, by organizing and advocating using Internet email, Evite, and text messaging, a true i-Generation transformation. Hallelujah!

January 6, 2012 FCS eBulletin
A Message from the Head

My arrival at school this morning was brightened, by a lengthy thank you letter (complete with photos) from one of our students; you may remember Naya Hutchinson's request for FCS families to support her family's annual winter coat collection for area residents.

Naya was amazed that FCS families responded so generously and noted that, "for the first time we had many coats for homeless children along with adults." The Hutchinson's holiday party included relatives, close friends, and some FCS families. They assembled sandwiches, baked cookies, sorted coats by size, collected hats, gloves, and scarves, and prepared all for distribution to needy District residents.

Meaningful, authentic work that truly benefits others. Many thanks to Naya and her family for bringing this project to us, and for the enthusiastic response from the FCS community.

In Peace,
Larry

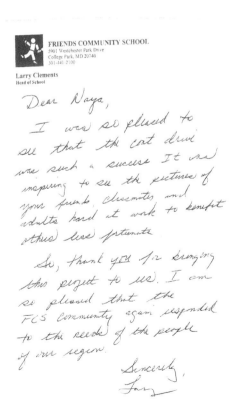

FRIENDS COMMUNITY SCHOOL
5901 Westchester Park Drive
College Park, MD 20740
301-441-2100

Larry Clements
Head of School

Dear Naya,

I was so pleased to see that the coat drive was such a success. It was inspiring to see the pictures of your friends, classmates and adults hard at work to benefit others less fortunate.

So, thank you for bringing this project to us. I am so pleased that the FCS community again responded to the needs of the people of our region.

Sincerely,
Larry

Case Study 3: Building the Restore Together Community.

Design of the Restore Together Community started on my knees in July of 2011, seeking guidance from the Holy Spirit to design and build that which God desired in the 21st century in order to restore God's marginalized and disenfranchised people in the new global Internet city. When the Holy Spirit revealed this Ark for the Remnant that God would have built, it would take me several weeks into August before I relinquished the overwhelming feeling of inadequacy to submit to the power of the almighty God to move forward with praying and designing, and praying and designing, and praying and designing for 75 days without ceasing. My spirit was consumed, I was constantly reminded that it is God's hand that controls power and might and it is at God's discretion that men and women are made great and given strength.[102] And so I was given vision (by the Holy Spirit) of how this community would be used for ministry. I was given the components, technical data structures, workflows and web design of this Ark that would need to be in place in order to provide the pieces for any combination or permutation of the physical, psychological, stewardship, and spiritual resources necessary for souls in need of psycho-spiritual wholeness; not only for themselves but the entire global urban community that is crying out for healing.

The first module of the Restore Together platform is the Community Organization and Activism module that facilitates the awakening and proclamation of the individual and collective prophetic voice, through mass planning and scheduling of one-to-one and one-to-many town hall chat communications that address social injustice. The second module is Crisis and Help, a resource that avails a database of organizations globally, such as food banks, shelters, AIDS clinics, hospitals, police stations, social services organizations, counseling resources, human trafficking assistance, substance and abuse organizations, etc., all for access to printable information, map directions and collaborative resources, real-time. The third module is Giving and Receiving,

---

102 1 Chronicles 29:11-12

which allows individuals, organizations, and corporations to give/ donate and request/receive products (food, shelter, clothing, etc.), services (legal, accounting, marketing, construction, administrative, counseling, etc.), funding (to organizations through grants, philanthropic giving, organizational matching, donations), gift cards (all companies that currently provide gifts cards) and commodities (electricity, gas, water, telecommunications, etc.) with receipt of tax documentation. The fourth module is the Counseling Consortium, which allows licensed counselors and ordained pastors to donate and provide counseling services to those in need through face-to-face, secure video chat or chat counseling sessions, and counseling best practices. The fifth module allows a LoveTap™, which is a newly-defined global text or shout about a selfless expression of sacrificial love or compassion for another human being with nodes displayed on a dynamic global map for reading encouragement by those inside and outside the Restore Together Community, constantly placing love in the atmosphere. The sixth and final module is the Restore Together App Store for developers who build and sell mobile apps that assist in the spiritual restoration of others. Within this module, individuals will also be able to download free apps and purchase apps that are for sale. Each member of the community will receive daily scripture of encouragement either random or subject-based need. The scripture will provide exegetical explanation, historical context and contemporary interpretation toward continuing discipleship. The entire community will allow each member to select language choice while in the community.

In October 2011, development was initiated for the case study portion of the Restore Together Community to include the Community Activism module, the Crisis Resources Module and the Counseling Consortium Module. In December, trademark and copyright applications were submitted both for the written work product, the website design, and all logos and graphics associated with Restore Together. In early January 2012, a 501 (3)(c) non-profit Restore Together, Inc. was established. In December of 2011, the Case Study Analysis for Restore Together was initiated for five different groups who were provided access to Restore Together and were asked a series of similar questions for conclusion and consolidation in January of 2012. The following is the outcome of that analysis:

Analysis 1

Title: i-Generation Mentoring Resource

Description: Assessment of Using Restore Together.com as a tool for building character when mentoring youth.

Participant: Libra Johnson, TV Host of In Transition – Rockville, Maryland and Director, Programs MENTOR: The National Mentoring Partnership – Alexandria, VA

Administrative Usage:
   On a scale of 1-10 (10 being the most helpful), please rate the following:
- Did you find the Restore Together Website user friendly and helpful? **10**
- Did you find the information on the Restore Together Website helpful? **10**

Productivity Increase:
   On a scale of 1-10 (10 being the most helpful), please rate the following:
- Could your projected productivity for your mission increase?
- Could your projected timeframe to achieve mission be accelerated? **9**

Projected Impact on Mission:
   Could Restore Together have a potential positive or negative impact on your mission?

Absolutely positive! MENTOR for example maintains a database of 5,000 mentoring programs and supports, with various products, services and research, 25 states offices and nearly a half a million mentoring relationships around the country. In my thinking a site like this has the potential to assist organizations like MENTOR, to reach its goal/mission of closing the mentoring gap and providing mentors to the 15 million children who still want and need a mentor.

Mentoring youth can be tough as so many of the youth that most need mentoring are considered "at-risk", and as a result are in great need of "wraparound" services. This site would be a very helpful tool for mentoring program staff, mentors and mentees. Quite often potential mentors are very intimidated by just the thought of having to be a role model and resource of knowledge meaningful experiences for their mentees. And as mentoring programs vary greatly in capacity and resources as well - attracting, training and retaining quality mentors is always a challenge.

This site would not only assist mentoring program managers in identifying meaningful activities for (mentor/mentee) matches that maximize the potential for mentee growth - academically socially and spiritually, but it could also be used during the required mentor training (minimum two hours pre-match training per the Elements of Effective Practice for Mentoring www.mentoring.org), to reassure mentors of their preparedness for the experience by introducing a resource they can use throughout the life of the match. And finally the mentee's development would be positively affected by making available to mentoring program managers and mentors, access to the services (counseling, etc.) their mentees most need for health and well-being. And further, access to Restore Together would empower the mentees directly by developing in them the habit of seeking assistance when needed for themselves, and giving back to others for a lifetime.

What aspects of Restore Together would be most beneficial (Community Activism, Crisis Resources, Counseling?) All of the above?

For the much needed wraparound services – all of the above!

Other Comments and Feedback:

1) What changes would need to be made to specifically serve the mentoring field? This I am not sure of but this is something to think about during development – there may be none.
2) Is there a mechanism so that a "member" can share/invite someone to experience Restore Together?
3) Is there a mechanism for (especially with youth population) video uploads for the sharing of video taken during the "giving" experience? This should be easy to forward as well.
4) I think something like a "Gratitude Wall" with two ways to view it:
   - one view where can see may dots all over the world where Restore Together members are working, sharing and giving in one view and;
   - second view where thank you notes (or love taps?) can be viewed from person to person, person to org, or org to org (a cell phone video thank you upload would also be great on this wall).
5) I think there should also be a way members can connect to each other, but I'm concerned if this works, is there a minimum age?
6) Will members receive a communication when they've uploaded something, been sent a message, or a request/inquiry has been responded to?

Analysis 2

Title: Christian Counseling Resource

Description: Assessment of Using Restore Together.com potential impact on Clinical and Pastoral Counseling.

Participant: Rev. Dr. Sherrill McMillan - Minister of Counseling and Family Services: Metropolitan Baptist Church - Washington DC. President of Garments Hem - Largo MD

Administrative Usage:

On a scale of 1-10 (10 being the most helpful), please rate the following:

- Did you find the Restore Together Website user friendly and helpful? **10**
- Did you find the information on the Restore Together Website helpful? **10**

Productivity Increase:

On a scale of 1-10 (10 being the most helpful), please rate the following:

- Did your projected productivity for your mission increase? **N/A**
- Was your projected timeframe to achieve mission accelerated? **N/A**

Projected Impact on Mission:

- Did Restore Together have a potential positive or negative impact on your mission? **N/A**
- What aspects of Restore Together were most beneficial (Community Activism, Crisis Resources, Counseling, All of the above? **N/A**

Other Comments and Feedback:

This will be an excellent source of help for clients and a valuable resource for counselors. It has the potential to increase the quality of the counseling experience while making it time-and cost effective.

Analysis 3

Title: Christian Counseling Resource

Description: Assessment of Using Restore Together.com's potential impact on pastoral counseling, effective/ essential out-reach (incidental and long term), community/environmental revitalization for children, youth and families.

Participant: Rev. Rudolph Waddy - Minister for Family Life - Ft. Washington Baptist Church, Fort Washington, MD

Administrative Usage:
On a scale of 1-10 (10 being the most helpful), please rate the following:
- Did you find the Restore Together Website user friendly and helpful? **10**
- Did you find the information on the Restore Together Website helpful? **10**

Productivity Increase:
On a scale of 1-10 (10 being the most helpful), please rate the following:
- Could your projected productivity for your mission increase? **10**
- Could your projected timeframe to achieve mission accelerate? **9**

Projected Impact on Mission:
Could Restore Together have a potential positive or negative impact on your mission?

Positive
What aspects of Restore Together were most beneficial (Community Activism, Crisis Resources, and Counseling, All of the above?

All of the above

Other Comments and Feedback:

Restore Together, in reality, is a very unique consortium of ministry/faith/community based services and resources that actualizes the problems and potential of the human condition on every level. In theory and deed, it provides easily assessable means for individual/

family/institutional restoration and prolonged support. Predictably, it demonstrates the power and promise of sowing and reaping by allowing users to deposit experiential knowledge and testimonial data into a shared residence thus, solidifying the credence and cogency of its designed mission. Without question, Restore Together is the missing pieces to the puzzle that connects equitable use of relational resources. It is a must-use resource for a perpetually evolving "I-generation" way of ministry and beyond.

Analysis 4

Title: Crisis and Help Resources

Description: Assessment of Using Restore Together.com as a Resource for homeless individuals and families in a homeless shelter community.

Participant: Chris Bramante - Community Outreach and Volunteer Coordinator - New Hope Housing Shelter - 8407 Richmond Hwy, Suite E, Alexandria, VA. 22309

Administrative Usage:
   On a scale of 1-10 (10 being the most helpful), please rate the following:
   Did you find the Restore Together Website user friendly and helpful? **10 – Very helpful and easy to use**
   Did you find the information on the Restore Together Website helpful? **10**

Productivity Increase: On a scale of 1-10 (10 being the most helpful), please rate the following:
   Did your projected productivity for your mission increase? **7**

Difficult to say; our residents are typically searching for employment, housing, and childcare—I think that when the website is complete, it will definitely assist in those searches.

Was your projected timeframe to achieve mission accelerated? **7**

Again, difficult to say—I would anticipate that the use of the completed website would make finding information for clients very easy and quick.

Projected Impact on Mission:

Did Restore Together have a potential positive or negative impact on your mission?

Positive—I think that both case managers and clients would be able to find resources and help very quickly.

What aspects of Restore Together were most beneficial (Community Activism, Crisis Resources, Counseling, All of the above?

Crisis resources are very helpful. I think the residents would take advantage of counseling services, and the community activism would be a nice forum for exchange of ideas with people in similar circumstances.

Other Comments and Feedback:

It will be helpful to have the sort function available for narrowing results on searches—to be able to sort by zip or city to find the resources nearby. It looks like the plan is there to have that function.

Analysis 5

Title: Crisis and Help Resources

Participant: Rev. Steven Johnson - Pastor - Abundant Faith Ministries - Baltimore Maryland

Description: Assessment of Using Restore Together.com as a Resource for unemployed congregants in need.

Administrative Usage:
On a scale of 1-10 (10 being the most helpful), please rate the following:
Did you find the Restore Together Website user friendly and helpful? **Yes (10)**
Did you find the information on the Restore Together Website helpful? **Yes (10)**

Productivity Increase:
On a scale of 1-10 (10 being the most helpful), please rate the following:
Did your projected productivity for your mission increase? **Yes (10)**
Was your projected timeframe to achieve mission accelerated? **Yes (10)**

Projected Impact on Mission:
Did Restore Together have a potential positive or negative impact on your mission?

A positive one; it made me look at the Ministry vision in a more global perspective. Secondarily, the realization that the vision will require more than just desire, technology must play an important role as well.

What aspects of Restore Together were most beneficial (Community Activism, Crisis Resources, Counseling, All of the above?

> All of the above; Pastors must use every resource at their disposal to get the message and mission out to the public. That will include the use of print media, databases and social networks. The message must be clear, concise and display all the service aspects that your ministry can offer. These steps will define and determine how impactful and far-reaching that your ministry will be.

Other Comments and Feedback:
Great project. Glad to have participated in the focus group.

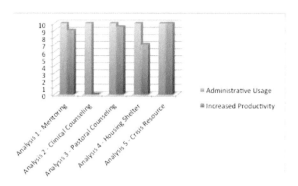

In summary, the average administrative usage was rated at a 10 and the average increased productivity was rated at 7.1 for Case Study 3. There were an average of three meetings with each analysis group/participant, during which they all received a clear overview of the Restore Together vision, website, and development timeline with instructions for filling out the self-explanatory questionnaire.

In the context of Case Study 1 – Organizing Community for Reconciliation, it was clear that the use of the Internet neutralized distant ministry resources to work toward recommendations and solutions resulting from a determined national collaboration, which planted the seed for future positive impact within the urban setting of the Nation's Capital. In Case Study 2 – i-Generation Transformation, use of collaborative technology allowed an 11-year old to feed 186 homeless people, and to clothe over 100 while learning to appreciate the power of giving and leadership. And in Case Study 3 – Building the Restore Together Community, a pastor, a television and National Mentor Association executive, a clinical counselor, a minister of family counseling, and a director of multiple homeless shelters were all enlightened to the potential power of technology-centered loving ministry in the midst of global urbanization.

CHAPTER SIX

Love

The sacrificial solution that will heal institutional sin such as oppression and poverty is at the very foundation of our existence. It is the most powerful thought ever conceived. It is simultaneously a noun, a verb, a pronoun, an adverb, an adjective, a preposition, a conjunction, and God's expectation of His creation. It is the very nucleus of who God is, what God does, and what God desires. The solution is the central and unending presence of one word, LOVE.

Now the Webster's dictionary has both a conditional and anemic definition of love. It says that love is: a strong affection for another arising out of kinship or personal ties like maternal love for a child (which is the Greek term *storge*); it says that love is: attraction based on sexual desire or affection and tenderness felt by lovers (which is the Greek term *eros*), and lastly it says that love is: affection based on admiration, benevolence, or common interests such as friendship and family (which is the Greek term *philia*). At best, Webster's dictionary is myopic, it places love in a box of circumstantial dependence, and conditional limitation. It is not reflective of love in the context of God. God's love knows no limitations. God's love cannot be placed in a box. God's love is compassionate, tough, patient, persevering, selfless, suffering, and victorious. God's love transforms, resurrects, and restores; God's love never fails.

Like Webster, we the church must be careful not to create an inadequate, convenient and comfortable definition of God's love. For if Webster took the time to truly and accurately address the definition of God's love, that one definition by itself would be infinite in length. That definition would be as extensive as the entire dictionary and would describe every combination and permutation of the Cross. For God's love is the Greek word *agape*, it is *caritas* or <u>unconditional</u>, it is absolute, it is eternal, and it is holistic and complete. God's love is not a weak passive love. It is love in action always seeking to preserve community, no matter the circumstance. It is an adaptive theology of positive social change. It is a global revolution of corrective morality. It is justification and declaration of peaceful and compassionate war against those oppressive activities that are antithetical to love, through confrontational love. God's love stretches out and touches the pathos, the deeper water, those that seem unreachable and untouchable.

Embedded within God's love is the Greek term *thelema* which means that God desires that we, those who were made in the image of God, reciprocate God's love and share it with one another no matter the circumstance. The church can no longer wait, as there is rapidly growing hate and evil; there are still children starving; there are still homeless waiting. While churches bicker internally over issues of stature, there are still abusive marriages, there are still dying people without healthcare, there are still naked waiting to be clothed, hungry waiting to be fed, and lame waiting to be commanded by God's servants to rise up and walk, through the power of the Holy Spirit. The world needs the church, perhaps like never before. The time and purpose for the church, independent of technology, economy or medium, is now: to show the world what love looks like!

In the new 21st century global urbanization, as the church awakens to take collaborative digitized and traditional action to restore all together, it must do so through love as described in 1 Corinthians Chapter 13 which states,

> Though I speak with the tongues of men and of angels, but have not love, I have become sounding brass or a clanging cymbal; 2And though I have the gift of prophecy, and understand all mysteries and all knowledge, and though I have all faith, so that I could

remove mountains, but have not love, I am nothing; ³And though I bestow all my goods to feed the poor, and though I give my body to be burned, but have not love, it profits me nothing; ⁴Love suffers long and is kind; love does not envy; love does not parade itself, is not puffed up; ⁵does not behave rudely, does not seek its own, is not provoked, thinks no evil; ⁶does not rejoice in iniquity, but rejoices in the truth; ⁷bears all things, believes all things, hopes all things, endures all things; ⁸Love never fails. But whether there are prophecies, they will fail; whether there are tongues, they will cease; whether there is knowledge, it will vanish away; ⁹For we know in part and we prophesy in part; ¹⁰ But when that which is perfect has come, then that which is in part will be done away; ¹¹ When I was a child, I spoke as a child, I understood as a child, I thought as a child; but when I became a man, I put away childish things; ¹² For now we see in a mirror, dimly, but then face to face. Now I know in part, but then I shall know just as I also am known; ¹³ And now abide faith, hope, love, these three; but the greatest of these is love.

Bibliography

Adler, P. A., & Adler, P. *The cyber worlds of self-injurers: Deviant communities, relationships, and selves*. Symbolic Interaction, 2008.

Ausburger, David. *The Freedom of Forgiveness*. Chicago: University of Chicago Press, 1993.

Baker, Don. *Beyond Forgiveness: The Healing Touch of Church Discipline*. Chicago: University of Chicago Press, 1999.

Barbour, Ian G. *Religion and Science: Historical and Contemporary Issues, Models and Paradigms*. New York, New York: Harper One, 1991.

Bonhoeffer, Dietrich. *Creation and Fall*. Minneapolis, Minnesota: Fortress Press, 2004.

Butler, Lee, H. Jr. *Liberating our Dignity, Saving our Souls*. Missouri: Chalice Press, 2006.

Censky, Annalyn. *Black Unemployment: Highest in 27 years*, September 2, 2011. CNN Money. http://money.cnn.com/2011/09/02/news/economy/black_unemployment_rate/ [accessed September 5, 2011]

Cole, David. *Can Our Shameful Prisons Be Reformed?* http://www.nybooks.com/articles/archives/2009/nov/19/can-our-shameful-prisons-be-reformed/ [accessed November 09, 2011]

Coleman, Butcher, Carson. *Psychology and Modern Life – Seventh Edition*. Dallas: Scott, Foresman and Company, 1984.

Collins, Gary R. *Christian Counseling A Comprehensive Guide*. United States: W Publishing Group, 1988.

Cone, James H. *Black Theology and Black Power*. Maryknoll: Orbis Books, 1997.

Cox, Harvey. *The Secular City: Toward a Theology of Social Change*. Toronto: Collier MacMillan, 1966.

Deshotels, T. H., & Forsyth, C. J. *Postmodern masculinities and the eunuch*. Deviant Behavior, 2007.

Dods, Marcus. *Saint Augustine: The City of God*. Peabody, Massachusetts: Hendrickson, 2010.

Fortune 500, September 15, 2011. http://money.cnn.com/magazines/fortune/fortune500/2009/snapshots/2608.html?source=story_f500_link [accessed October 15, 2011]

Freire, Paulo. *Pedagogy of the Oppressed*. New York, New York: The Continuum International Publishing Group Inc., 2009.

Gunderson, Gary. *Boundary Leaders: Leadership Skills for People of Faith*. Minneapolis: Fortress Press, 2004.

Joinson, A. N. *Deviance and the Internet: New Challenges for Social Science*. Social Science Computer Review, 2005.

Khan, Huma. *Congress Mulls Cuts to Food Stamps Program Amid Record Number of Recipients*, ABC News, May 31, 2011.

King, Martin Luther Jr., *The Essential Writings and Speeches of Martin Luther King, Jr.* New York, New York: Harper Collins, 1986.

Kornfeld, Margaret. *Cultivating Wholeness: A Guide to Care and Counseling in Faith Communities*. New York: Continuum, 2006.

Levy. Dan and Prashant Gopal, Foreclosure Filings in U.S. May Jump 20% From Record 2010 as Crisis Peaks, January 13, 2011, Bloomberg. http://www.bloomberg.com/news/2011-01-13/u-s-foreclosure-filings-may-jump-20-this-year-as-crisis-peaks.html [accessed November 09, 2011]

McGuire, Meredith B. *Religion: The Social Context*. Illinois: Waveland Press, 2002.

Moltmann, Jürgen. *God in Creation*. Minneapolis, Minnesota: Fortress Press, 1993.

_____. *The Way of Jesus Christ*. Minneapolis, Minnesota: Fortress Press, 1993.

Mumford, Lewis. *The City in History*. Orlando, Florida: Harcourt Inc., 1989.

National Alliance to End Homelessness. *Increases in Homelessness on the Horizon*, September 28, 2011. http://www.

endhomelessness.org/content/article/detail/4226[accessed October 15, 2011]

Niebuhr, Reinhold. *Moral Man and Immoral Society: A Study in Ethics and Politics*. Louisville: Westminster John Knox Press, 2001.

Nkrumah, Kwame. *Neo-Colonialism, the Last Stage of Imperialism*. London: Thomas Nelson & Sons, Ltd., 1966. http://www.marxists.org/subject/africa/nkrumah/neo-colonialism/

Peters, Ronald E. *Urban Ministry: An Introduction*. Nashville, Tennessee: Abingdon Press, 2007.

Pew Forum on Religion and Public Life: *U.S. Religious Landscape Survey* http://religions.pewforum.org/reports [accessed November 09, 2011]

Poverty Facts and Stats, http://www.globalissues.org/article/26/poverty-facts-and-stats [accessed November 09, 2011]

Reeve, C.D.C. *Plato Republic*. Indianapolis, Indiana: Hacket Publishing Company, 1992.

Rice, Jesse. *The Church of Facebook: How the Hyperconnected Are Redefining Community*. Colorado Springs, Colorado: David C. Cook, 2009.

Rogers, Marc M., Smoak, Natalie, N., Liu, Jiu. *Self-reported deviant computer behavior. Deviant Behavior: a big-5, moral choice, and manipulative exploitive behavior analysis*. Indiana: Routledge Taylor and Francis Group, 2006.

Rosen, Larry D. Understanding the iGeneration and the Way They Learn. New York: Palgrave Macmillan, 2010.

Rosenbaum, Dottie. *The Food Stamp Program is Growing to Meet Need*. Center on Budget and Policy Priorities, July 12, 2006. http://www.cbpp.org/cms/index.cfm?fa=view&id=460 [accessed October 15, 2011]

Schutlze, Quentin. *Communicating for Life: Christian Stewardship in Community and Media*. Grand Rapids, Michigan: Baker Academic a Division of Baker Publishing Group, 2007.

Thurman, Howard. *Jesus and the Disinherited*. Boston, Massachusetts: Beacon Press, 1996.

United Press International, House Wants to Cut Food Stamps, http://www.arcamax.com/health/healthtips/s-917916-690577 [accessed October 15, 2011]

U.S. Census. *Income, Poverty, and Health Insurance Coverage in the United States: 2009*, U.S. Census.gov, http://www.census.gov/prod/2010pubs/p60-238.pdf [accessed October 15, 2011]

USDA. Supplemental Nutrition Assistance Program (SNAP): *Number of Persons Participating Nationally and by State* http://www.fns.usda.gov/pd/29SNAPcurrPP.htm [accessed October 15, 2011]

Watson, Debra. *The Dramatic Effect of Poverty on Death Rates in the US*, http://www.wsws.org/articles/2011/jul2011/pove-j13.shtml [accessed November 09, 2011]

West, Cornell. *Prophesy Deliverance! An African American Revolutionary Christianity.* Louisville, Kentucky: Westminster John Knox Press, 2002.

Wheeler, Sondra. *Ethics – Formative Influences in the Christian Moral Tradition.* Class Notes, Wesley Theological Seminary: Washington, DC, 19 September 2007.

Young, Josiah. *Barth: The Genesis Emphasis.* Lecture, Wesley Theological Seminary: Washington DC, February 7, 2007.